GOLF

Alan Fine

Published by InsideOut Development LLC
95 N 490 W
American Fork
Utah 84003
U.S.A.

First published 1993
Reprinted 1994, 1999
© Alan Fine, 2006
The moral right of the author has been asserted.

ISBN 0 9672530-0-4

Designed by George Knight
Illustrations by Dave F. Smith

CONTENTS

Foreword

This book is a product of the meeting of two empty minds (and two very large noses). For the record, 12 years ago, Alan's mind was a lot more empty than mine, this of course being a good thing. Through the years I played this absurd sport for a living, I found that the lessons Alan taught me were just as useful in my everyday life as they were in golf. If you want to learn about anything, the best way to do it is to pay attention. This book will teach you to pay attention, so sit up straight, damnit!

My fellow Ulsterman, Van Morrison, pretty much summed up this book in the song "I Forgot That Love Existed":

> If my heart could do my thinking,
> and my head began to feel,
> I could look upon the world and you,
> and know what's truly real.

So either read this book, or buy the album *A Night In San Francisco*.

David Feherty
CBS Golf Analyst
Former Ryder Cup Golfer

ABOUT THE AUTHOR

Alan Fine was a member of the Professional Tennis Coaches Association of Great Britain. His interest in how people learn and perform under pressure has led him to advise athletes in a variety of sports, from Davis Cup tennis players (Buster Mottram—former British No. 1), to Ryder cup golfers (Colin Montgomerie—World No. 3) and to David Feherty (now a CBS commentator), to squash players (Phil Kenyon—former World No. 5) and fencers (British Olympic foil team).

He has authored two books: *Play to Win Golf* (with David Feherty) and *InsideOut Golf* (formerly *Mind Over Golf*, published by the BBC). As a result of his success with athletes, Alan has been asked by executives and business leaders to apply the same principles within their organizations. His performance models are used and have been institutionalized by many companies worldwide. His work is focused on improvement methods that are simple, user friendly, actionable under pressure and deliver measurable results.

As the founding partner of InsideOut Development, Alan speaks to and consults with leaders and managers of world-class companies, helping organizations and individuals improve their performance. His clients include IBM, Procter & Gamble, KPMG, DuPont, AT&T, Sun Microsystems, Carlson Companies, BellSouth, and Nationwide Insurance.

ACKNOWLEDGEMENTS

So many people have helped and continue to help me increase my understanding of performance. But it is right that I give special mention to a few of them:

To my dear wife Penny, whose special insight and encouragement never cease to brighten my life.

To George Knight, who has pulled this edition together in the way only George can.

To Gary Cullen (ex-PGA European Tour Professional), whose fault it is that I ever became involved in golf—happy fishing, Gary!

To all the long-suffering golfers I have been lucky enough to work with, many of whom have become good friends, and especially David Feherty, Richard Boxall, David Llewellyn, Phillip Price, and Stephen Ames, who also allowed me to write about our work together.

And last but not least, to my two children. When I was writing this book they were both too young to have any idea of how much they were (and still are) teaching me about learning!

PREFACE

We hear people talk more and more about the importance of the mind in golf. I tend to be one of the biggest culprits; I'm fascinated by the dilemmas the game continually produces. Why is it that we fear short putts? Why do some people freeze when they have to play over water? What drives us to make a mess of a relatively simple shot at a crucial stage in a match? And why is it that we are able to hit the ball well on the practice ground, but never play as well in competition as we know we can?

These phenomena—and there are many others—cannot be explained in purely physical terms. We spend much of our time learning about the theory of swinging a golf club, yet we lack the self-control to be able to put that knowledge into practice. The point at which we recognize this is usually the point at which we consider learning about and improving our mental skills.

As spectators, it is often the mental side of golf that gives us such drama and excitement. The Ryder Cup matches have perhaps proved more than anything else that at the highest level, golf is a game of mental control. Even the world's greatest players feel the strain. Some crack under the pressure of intense competition, while others seem to thrive on a challenge and shift up a gear when the heat is on.

Few of us ever perform up to the level of our true potential for more than a brief period of time. We might play the odd good shot, or produce a good round once in a while, but we find it hard to sustain our performance over any given length of time. The game we play against ourselves is much more difficult than the one we play against the golf course. We hit great shots some of the time, and it's these that keep us going when our game won't come together.

I'm not a professional golfer, and in this book I will not attempt to teach you the technical or physical skills necessary to play the game. They are covered in more than enough detail elsewhere. What I will talk about are some of the things I have found to be important in learning and performing these skills.

Throughout my career I have been increasingly fascinated by how we can make learning more effective and more enjoyable. I was a tennis coach for 15 years, and during that time I became interested in the work of Timothy Gallwey, whose books *The Inner Game of Tennis* and *The Inner Game of Golf* have brought the mental game into prominence. To me, his work opened the door to applying some of the psychological theories I had been studying and led me to many other interesting new approaches.

Golf: The agony...

Over the last twenty years I have been privileged to work with many professionals from the European and USPGA tours, including David Feherty, Richard Boxall, David Llewellyn, Colin Montgomerie, Phillip Price, and Stephen Ames—golfers who have through their own experiences recognized the importance of developing their mental skills. They have patiently watched me learn—sometimes at their expense, other times at their gain—and this book is based on all these experiences.

This is not an instruction book covering everything you need to know to play golf! It does not tell you how to swing the club. And it does not claim that if you do all of the things contained within its pages you will take ten strokes off your handicap. It does, however, contain some things that have been helpful to many golfers, both amateur and professional. These things have been helpful in the sense that some of the golfers have found that they enjoy playing the game much more, find it easier and less stressful to learn the skills they need, and most of all, play better.

I believe that the missing link to reaching our true potential has largely to do with improving our mental approach to the game. It is not all there is to being a good golfer, but with good mental skills, we have our best chance of playing to our full potential.

...and the ecstasy of the Ryder Cup

KEY POINTS — CHAPTER ONE

- A major part of golf is mental.

- We don't practice mental skills in proportion to how important we think they are.

- Reasons for this include:
  Being obsessed with technique;
  Avoiding "mental things";
  Our ignorance of the way we learn.

- Reading this won't make you play better, only taking action will.

Golf Is a Mental Game

H ow much of your golf do you think is mental? When I have posed this question to individuals and groups I have worked with, the usual response is that golf is at least 80 percent mental. I've never had an estimate lower than 50 percent.

What intrigues me most about the answers I receive isn't what the exact percentage is (of course there is no statistical validity to these answers), but that people actually do attribute such importance to the mental side of the game. From their collective experiences, these golfers—both amateurs and professionals alike—are saying they consider the mental side of the game to be highly important in terms of their overall performance, and at least as important as their swings. I then ask how much of their practice time they spend deliberately rehearsing and developing their mental skills? So far I have not met anyone who has said they devote more than 5 percent of their total practice time to improving their mental skills.

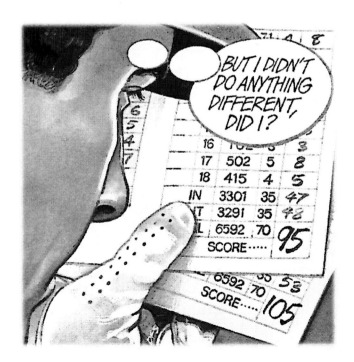

95 one day, 105 the next ...

So let's add it up. On average, less than 5 percent of our effort is directed toward a part of the game that is generally regarded as contributing at least 50 percent toward our overall performance on the golf course. Although we may recognize and appreciate the significance of the mental skills, most of our practice time is devoted to developing technical skills, i.e., analyzing and fine-tuning the swing. Something doesn't add up here.

GOLF: THE DILEMMAS OF THE MIND

At whatever level we play golf, our performance on the course is determined by what our mind does. Think about it. You can play to your handicap one day, and yet you're 15 over the next; you can hit the ball consistently on the practice ground, but not out on the course when it most counts in competition; you can use all the clubs in your bag except, say, the 4-iron; you usually play well around your home course, but for some reason always seem to make a mess of the 14th hole; you have no problem with putts of 10 or 15 feet, but become anxious over a relatively simple 3-footer; you can chip perfectly well around the green, but always duff the ball when you face a shot over a bunker.

Despite the wealth of technical knowledge available to us, and our eagerness to analyze and work on our swings, we still wrestle with the frustration of playing reasonably well one day, but terribly the next. While we might go out and shoot 95 on Saturday morning, on Sunday afternoon we can do no better than 105, even though we are playing on the same course, with the same clubs, under the same weather conditions, and with the same partner(s).

Whether we like it or not, our performance is determined by our mental state, or as Timothy Gallwey describes it in his book *The Inner Game of Golf*, the game that is played within the mind—the "Inner Game." As the great amateur Bobby Jones implied many years ago, a lot is to be gained if we can learn to control the workings of our mind when we're out on the golf course, i.e., improve our mental skills.

MENTAL STRENGTH

Watch the top pros on the tour and you will see they all swing in different ways. So what do they have in common? One thing is that they all return the clubhead to the ball in a repeatable fashion. While their swings reflect obvious physical differences, they are all remarkably similar at impact—and that's where it counts. And they can all get the ball into the hole in relatively few strokes. Of course, some do

"Competitive golf is played mainly on a 5$^{1}/_{2}$ inch course,... the space between your ears."
—*Bobby Jones*

this more successfully than others, and it is usually the difference you cannot see that sorts out the winners from losers. Just as in life generally, the top performers in golf are those players who are very strong mentally.

One of the characteristics of a truly successful golfer is that he can still perform reasonably well even when his swing is a little awry. When you hear commentators describe someone as a "tough competitor," it's usually a reference to that player's ability to keep a score going, even though he's not really striking the ball particularly well. People often describe players like Faldo, Norman, and Woods, arguably some of the best golfers in the world, as great examples of players who are mentally "tough." Another would be Jack Nicklaus, who in his prime had legendary powers of concentration. When it mattered most, he was able to focus only on what he was doing to the extent that he literally blanked out everything else around him.

If you were to follow the scores of the mentally tough competitors throughout the season, you would find that rarely do they shoot scores of more than one or two over par, at worst. These golfers suffer peaks and slumps like everyone else, but they are so strong mentally that they are able to survive periods of physical weakness (i.e., days when

Tiger Woods and Ernie Els,- two of golf's toughest competitors

their swings are slightly off key) on the strength of their belief in themselves and their desire to succeed. As a result, their scoring range is likely much tighter than that of the golfer who does not have such capabilities.

It seems to be an annual tradition in the open championships for an unknown player to lead the field at the end of the first round, and although he might have scored a 65 on the opening day, he usually follows it up with a much higher score on Friday, when the enormousness of the occasion hits him squarely between the ears.

At the highest level, it is simply the power of the mind that separates the winners from the losers. During the closing holes of a major championship, it is not the leading player's swings that come under the microscope—those players have all proved they can play—it is their mental strength and their ability to withstand pressure that become the deciding factor.

IT'S ALL IN THE MIND

Because of the dynamics of golf, the effects of the mental part of the game are more graphic than in most sports. In fact, the effects of anything you do are magnified greatly, and in that respect golf is much

All good golfers return the clubhead to the ball in a repeatable way, e.g., Phillip Price (left) and Stephen Ames.

less forgiving toward changes in your mental and physical state than
most other sports. The slightest change physically can have a major
effect on the outcome, and the precision that's necessary to produce
a good shot is phenomenal when you consider the physics involved.
The clubhead travels a distance of at least 20 feet during a typical
swing, yet if the club face is only a fraction of an inch open at the
moment of impact, the result is a shot that could be as much as fifty
yards off line. Tiny changes in what the club does are indiscernible
to us, and so we often cannot tell what it is we are doing differently. Our swings feel the same, yet they produce consecutive results
that are very different.

The unique pace of the game is another factor that contributes
to its mental demands. In the four hours or so that we spend on the
golf course, only three or four minutes are actually spent swinging
the club and executing a shot. The rest of the time we are free to
think, to get worried, to become anxious and generally lose concentration.

In reflex sports, such as tennis, we are much more reactive and
our mind is not given the opportunity to indulge in as much self-
sabotage. But in golf—a game in which we always initiate the
action—there is simply too much time to think. We think about
our technique, about what we should and shouldn't be doing; we
worry about the trouble that awaits us on the next hole and dwell
on the three putts we just took on the previous one. In other words,
our minds are continually busy, and our concentration is therefore
adversely affected.

THE MIND GAME—THE AREA OF GREATEST GAIN

Looking at the development of sport over the last thirty or forty
years, we can see a trend toward technical and physical excellence.
Athletes today are more fit than they have ever been before. They
use improved training methods, they have the benefit of much
improved analysis and feedback mechanisms, and they eat scientifi-
cally devised diets. The net result, not surprisingly, is that our athletes are altogether fitter and stronger and technically more profi-
cient than their predecessors, and their performances are pushing
the limits of human endeavor ever further. In fact, they are pushing
so hard that we now frequently encounter drug abuse in the sometimes desperate search for higher performance. However, it is the
mental skills or psychology that provides us with the area where we
can really make the biggest gains, because we actually still know so
little.

"The mental and physical ... are inextricably linked."
—David Leadbetter

19

The greatest mind of them all?

Even the greatest of golfers are susceptible to lapses in concentration. The 1981 British Open at Royal St. George's was won by the little-known American Bill Rogers, but the early headlines were taken by Jack Nicklaus, who in the first round shot a 13-over par score of 83, his worst performance ever in a major championship. It later transpired that Nicklaus had been told only minutes before he was due to tee off that one of his sons was ill at home. That news had naturally unsettled him, but his professional pride stood in the way of making excuses, and to an astonished gathering of pressmen, the man who many regard as the world's greatest ever golfer explained that his 83 was "the best I could do today—I tried on every single shot."

It is simply a measure of his phenomenal playing ability—coupled with an incredible desire and absolute belief in himself—that, having satisfied himself of his son's condition, Nicklaus went out the next day and shot a course record of 66.

Every physical action we perform is controlled by the brain. In fact, it is impossible to separate the mental and physical aspects of our makeup—we would need a lobotomy to do that—so why then do we tend to neglect such an important aspect of the game?

OUR OBSESSION WITH TECHNIQUES

More has been written about how to swing a golf club than almost any other human activity. Every month, volumes are produced, breaking down the swing into minute parts; books and videos meticulously detail what we need to do to play well. To me, it seems that almost every conceivable movement in the swing has already been described. And it's all sound stuff! But if all it took to play well was the ability to understand what to do, we would all be on the Ryder Cup team.

Much of our obsession with technique stems from thinking that the more we know, the better we will be able to do it. We frequently work on our swings in the same way that a mechanic would dismantle an engine. We buy videos, read books and magazines, and discuss our swings with other players. We believe that if we hit it perfectly, or hit it like Els or Woods, we will play perfectly, yet there's little evidence of a correlation between the perfect strike and the perfect score, particularly at the top level.

I remember speaking to David Llewellyn during a European tour event. He had shot 76 in his first round and couldn't understand why—"I struck the ball really well, but all I could do was a 76." The following day he shot 68 and said, "I didn't deserve it. I played like a dog." Evidently, being able to reproduce a perfect strike or swing doesn't necessarily equate with being able to produce a perfect score. Ironically, while most of professional golfers will admit that building a classic swing and searching for the perfect strike isn't necessarily what golf's all about, it's what they spend all of their practice time working for.

(opposite) Jack Nicklaus during the first round of the 1981 British Open.

David Llewellyn "played like a dog" and scored 68.

PSYCHO-SICK

"There's nothing wrong with me. Why do I need to see a psychologist?"

This is a comment I have overheard on many occasions. For many people, to be seen working on their mental skills is tantamount to admitting that there's something wrong with them. This attitude prevails in spite of the fact that many well-known professional golfers, not to mention successful athletes in other fields, openly publicize the fact that it has helped them. Some people would rather not let anyone else know that they work on their mental game.

But think about it. If we're unwell, we go to see a doctor. And if we are keen to get physically fit, we seek the advice of an exercise physiologist. The same logic applies if we want to become mentally fit. If we are mentally sick, we see a psychiatrist, but if we want to become super-fit mentally, we seek the help of a sports psychologist.

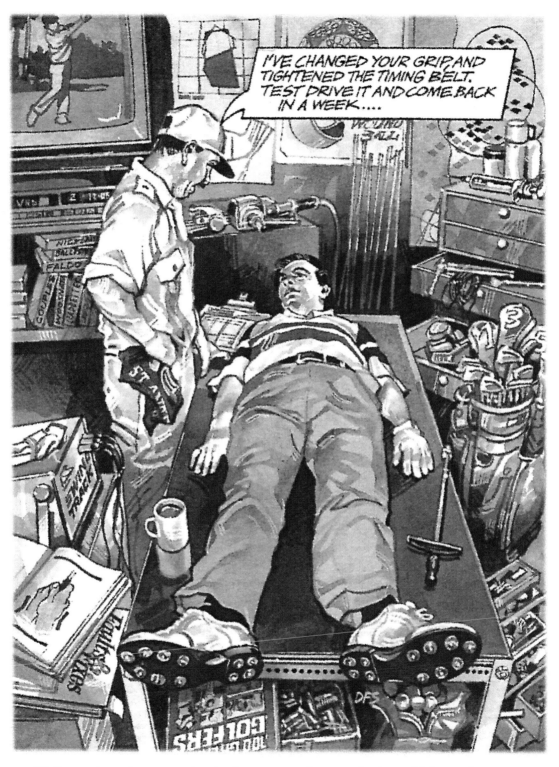

We frequently work on our swings in the same way that a mechanic would dismantle an engine.

TEACHER-CENTERED LEARNING

Sometimes the way we are taught is a factor in making it difficult to perform. I'll give you an example.

I started my career as a tennis coach. One of the problems I encountered regularly was this: I would instruct some people how to play a particular shot, let's say a backhand, and they would do just as I asked. I would give other people exactly the same instruction and it seemed to make them worse! And yet I knew it was the correct instruction, so I would tell them again and give them even more instructions. And they would get even worse. They were so busy thinking about all the things they had to do to play the backhand that the ball had gone by before they even started their swing. So then I would decide that they just weren't cut out to play the game. In other words, it was their fault!

I was wrong. The problem was not theirs, it was mine. I was so obsessed with my way of doing things on the tennis court that I wasn't interested in how my pupils learned. My lessons centered around what I as a teacher wanted them to do, not what they as students needed to be able to learn effectively.

If you have had golf lessons from a number of different professionals, you have probably had a similar experience in some of those lessons.

What opened my eyes was applying one of the techniques Timothy Gallwey talks about in his Inner Game books. I had been teaching a nine year-old girl for about six weeks. In that time her best

The effect of our thinking on our behavior—and consequently on our performance—can be illustrated by this simple experiment. Take a piece of string between 12 and 18 inches (30 and 45 cm) long, attach a weight, such as a large paper clip, to one end, and hold it out in front of your body. Then, keeping the weight as steady as possible, picture in your mind the paper clip moving back and forth in a simple pendulum movement. If you have vividly imagined the pendulum motion, you will find that the paper clip has begun to move in exactly the way you had imagined even though you thought you were keeping it steady. (Now imagine it moving in counterclockwise circles.) In other words, whatever you think about will be represented physically in some way. So whenever you say to yourself, "Don't go in the water on the right..."

back-and-forth rally with me on the practice court was just six consecutive strokes. I had kept the technical instruction very simple for her because she didn't seem to be particularly coordinated, and it had taken her several half-hour lessons to get even this far.

Sensing that my normal method of coaching was proving difficult for her to follow, I decided to try out one of Gallwey's techniques. I asked her to forget everything I had told her so far, and instead simply say "bounce" out loud every time the ball bounced on the court, and "hit" every time the ball hit her racket. The results were astonishing. She hit 53 consecutive shots in her first rally. She was thrilled, her mother had almost fallen off her seat, and I was furious! I didn't understand why this had worked, and I was confused as to why what I had taught her up to now had had so little effect in comparison.

STOP! WARNING!

Reading this book will not make you a better golfer! In fact, reading any book will not make you a better golfer. We all know people who seem to have read every word ever written on golf and yet who have made little—if any—improvement.

If you think that simply by reading this book you will become a better golfer, then you will be disappointed. While the subject and content of the following chapters will center around developing the mental skills, you still need to understand the physical techniques of the game. But you can get that from many good sources. This book is based on the notion that in our search for bodily control—which is the essence of golf—we must complement our need for technical instruction with increased mental awareness. Only when we can harness the two will we likely improve significantly.

The purpose of this book is to provide some insight into the mental aspects of playing this addictive game. And by the way, only **doing** the exercises and suggestions will make any difference. Just reading them won't!

Bounce-hit?

In his book The Inner Game of Tennis, *Timothy Gallwey explains the concept of "bounce-hit," a concentration exercise that he found greatly improved the performance and accelerated the learning rate of tennis players.*

The pupil was asked to say out loud the word "bounce" as the approaching ball landed, and "hit" when he felt the ball make contact with the racket. The object of the exercise was simply to maintain sensory contact with the ball and to say "bounce-hit," "bounce-hit" aloud with as much accuracy as possible—"bounce" when the ball landed, and "hit" when he struck it with his racket. Gallwey noted that the more attention given to saying "bounce" and "hit," the less his students consciously thought about their technique and the more successful they were in returning the ball. It allowed their subconscious to let them do what they already knew how to. (A comparable "back-hit" exercise for golf is described on page 95.) Later I began to understand how the exercise regulated the mental state and that the mental state drives the physical action. I had made my first steps towards "student-centered" learning.

KEY POINTS — CHAPTER TWO

- The brain drives what we do physically.
- Mental skills enable us to perform the technical skills.
- Our response to any given situation is determined by how we perceive reality accurately.
- Mental interference prevents us from accurately perceiving reality.
- Intensifying our experience reduces interference, increases our learning, and improves our performance.

Mental Skills

All of us have a mental state that affects our performance. The more we can develop our skill at controlling that mental state, the better we will perform all our other skills.

WHAT ARE MENTAL SKILLS?

Mental skills are the internal skills that enable us to perform successfully the technical skills (physical skills) we have already stored within our subconscious, or to learn those new skills we wish to store in our subconscious. Examples of these mental skills are concentration (our ability to focus our attention), energy control (being "pumped-up" or "psyched-up"), self-confidence (self-belief), and our ability to use our imagination effectively (the ability to visualize). The degree of skill we have in each of these specific areas is reflected in our body language and in the words we use, but most of all, it is reflected in our physical performance.

We use our mental skills in every minute of our lives. In whatever we do it is our brain that drives our behavior; therefore, our brain is responsible for our performance. Our brain "houses" the mental skills we have; it sorts and interprets the stimuli we receive through our senses—i.e., what we see, hear and feel; and on the basis of this interpretation, the brain drives what we do physically.

What most people fail to realize is that it is possible to train these inner skills. In the same way that we can design specific exercises to help us improve our swing technique, we can devise ways to improve our mental skills, and as a result improve our performance. In fact, it's sometimes easier to improve our mental skills than our physical skills. The exercises shown later in this book can be practiced off the golf course as well as on it.

THE BRAIN AND PERFORMANCE

In golf it is very easy to get caught up in the purely technical aspects of the game. Although it is essential that we apply some quality practice in this area, if that is all we do, we ignore what it is that

Our brain controls everything we do.

controls our technique. It's like spending all our spare time and money on building a high-performance sports car, using all the latest technology and tuning it to perfection, only to let a monkey take the controls and drive it on the road when it really matters. When we fail to learn the basic mental skills in golf, we do the equivalent of allowing a monkey to drive our swings—and we occasionally see this reflected in our behavior out on the golf course!

Our brain controls everything we do. As far as I can tell, it is not possible to split golf into separate mental and physical elements. The two are so inextricably linked that whenever we deal with one we have no choice but to deal with the other. To improve our performance in any activity, it can be enormously helpful to understand how our brain works, and what we can do to make it work more efficiently. The more we understand the mechanism by which we learn and perform, the better equipped we will be to cope with the information we have to deal with and act upon.

LEARNING

In my search for clues to improving performance, I have found it helpful to think about learning and performance in different ways. As yet we know so little about how our brains work that it isn't possible to be definitive; suffice it to say that different people relate to words and concepts in differing ways (we will discuss this in more detail later). The following descriptions show the way I currently see the process of learning and performance unfolding.

Learning, Understanding or Both

One of the most common blocks to learning I am familiar with is the confusion that surrounds the difference between "learning" and "understanding." Often, what happens in golf is that we confuse understanding what to do with the ability to act on or implement that understanding. In other words, we tend to believe that the more we understand the "what to do," the more we will have learned and the more we will be "able" to do.

The "what to do" in golf is the mass of information available to us on how to play the game—the detailed theory first explains all the body movements necessary to return the club face to the ball in the most effective way. But simply reading and understanding this information—whether it's describing the grip, the posture or the back-swing—is very different from actually being able to do it. Learning is not simply understanding; learning is experiencing a concept to the point of being able to execute that concept—that's how it becomes a skill.

Think about it this way. A pilot could explain to us how to fly an airplane, but while we might understand what he is saying, we certainly won't have learned how to fly. The only way we will ever do that is to get out and physically experience what is involved.

If we confuse learning with understanding, when we find we are unable to perform as we would ideally like to, we are inclined to go off in search of more "how to" instruction. We want to know exactly what it is we are doing wrong and what we need to do to put it right. However, most of us already have all the technical information we will

" It is not the player who knows where the club should be who is successful; it is the player who knows where the club is. "

David Feherty
(pre-1991 Ryder Cup)

The Description is NOT the Experience

Imagine that you are training for a parachute jump. You've been to the classes, and you've read all there is to read about parachuting. Yet you still have no idea of what it is like to actually do it. It is impossible to know without doing it because words cannot give you the experience. So it is with golf.

ever need in order to play well (some of us have too much, others have the wrong information, and some both). It is not that we don't understand what to do, it is simply that we are not sufficiently skilled in acting on the information we have.

Learning Is Inbuilt

Psychologists tell us that we learn in our first five years half of what we learn in our whole lifetime. So why does our rate of learning slow down so much after these first few years?

As children we had a tremendous capacity and appetite to learn; it was inbuilt at birth and is part of being human. We experienced the first years of our lives without preconceived ideas about what was right or wrong, or good or bad, or what we should or should not do. We had little or no fear or inhibition. During our formative years we developed our basic motor-skills through a very natural process, one that was free of formal instruction or training. We learned how to walk and to talk, to eat with a knife and fork, to run up and down stairs, and so on.

When we attempt something as young children, our reaction is along the lines of "Oh, that's what happens. That's interesting. I wonder what happens if I try to do it this way..." We are inquisitive. We do not judge our performances other than to decide what to do differently the next time in order to get what we wanted. Everything we do is new and exciting. Our minds are relaxed, and learning is fun.

The way in which children learn is epitomized in their reaction to failure. When a child falls while learning to walk, he doesn't react by saying to himself, "You dummy, you fell over. Why don't you try to keep your head still and keep your balance. Come on, try harder." Children don't recognize failure. They just pick themselves up and try again.

Then somewhere between the age of about five and seven years, we begin to understand the concepts of right and wrong, good and bad, should and shouldn't. As a result we focus a lot of our energy and attention on avoiding the "bad," the "wrong" and the "shouldn'ts," because we find that the consequences of these can be painful, or threaten us in some way. Our efforts are now directed into avoiding failure as distinct from learning.

By the time we reach adulthood, many of us are so fixated on there being a right and wrong way of doing things that we end up blocking our natural ability. We judge and evaluate our performance against some blueprint we think will fix the problem. The potential for learning remains within us all, but as we grow older we tend to adopt a very analytical "left-brained" approach to learning (see Chapter Three) which actually slows down the process of improving.

You are probably familiar with the symptoms. Our minds become so full of complicated and confusing instructions (keep your grip pressure light... keep your head still... turn your shoulders,... etc.) that we stifle our natural instincts and distort our perception of what's really happening as we are trying to play. If we had tried to follow similarly detailed instructions when we were children learning to walk, or ride a bicycle, it would have been much less effective.

And yet this is exactly how we go about learning to play golf, and in doing so, we eliminate that invaluable period of trial and error without the pressure of evaluation, or having to do it right. This is the most valuable part of the learning process—a time of working things out for ourselves and attaching feelings and meanings to our perceptions and actions.

Is Golf Natural?

People have often said to me, "But surely you have to do this analysis. After all, the golf swing is not a natural thing to do." Well, no and yes. No, you don't need all that information (but you do need some), and yes, golf isn't natural. *But learning is.* It is an inbuilt mechanism that exists in all of us, and the more we understand about how each of us likes to learn, the easier it will be to accelerate our learning and improve our results.

PERCEPTION: THE KEY TO LEARNING AND PERFORMANCE

It is through our perception that we know there is a world out there. We gather detailed information about our surroundings through our senses—i.e., what we see, hear, feel, taste and smell. That's how we make sense of the world in which we live and what we do in it. Similarly, we are aware of what we do on the golf course by seeing, feeling and hearing (taste and smell don't have much relevance in golf—at least not until the 19th hole!). We see the ball at our feet, for example; we observe the shape of the hole, the position of the bunkers and the proximity of the trees. We feel the way in which our bodies move before, during and after a shot, and we feel the wind and wonder how it will affect our stroke. At the same time, we hear the swish of the club as it swings through the air, and we hear the voices of other people.

Stairclimbing—
Read with Care

Most of as have climbed stairs two at a time without any problem. We have also experienced those occasions when for some reason we thought about what we were doing, hesitated and then stumbled. We can do it easily and automatically all the time until we begin to think about it.

I think, therefore I do.

All these senses are external to us, but we also have an internal world that we see, hear and feel. We each have a set of beliefs based on our expectations of future events, and on memories of past events when we were in a similar situation. And just as the external stimuli we experience will have an effect on our interpretation of any given situation, so these internal stimuli shape our perception and therefore our reaction.

In our mind we see our prediction of the events to come or our memories of the past. For example, we think about what will happen to the shot after we strike the ball, or about what happened the last time we were in a similar situation. When we stand on the first tee at our home course we might see what we hope will happen—the ball flying straight up the middle of the fairway; or we may see what we fear might happen—the ball disappearing into the trees, as happened last time.

Similarly, we feel our prediction of the events to come or our memories of the past. We might feel the smoothness of our swing or the elation in response to a good shot; if we anticipate a poor shot, we might feel uncomfortable or awkward over the ball, or disappointed. We also hear our prediction of the events to come or our memories of the past. If we anticipate success, we might hear the crack of the ball as it is met squarely and forcefully by the clubface; if we anticipate failure, that sound might be a muffled thud as the club strikes the ground behind the ball.

In golf there are infinite varieties of sights, sounds, and feelings that we experience whenever we are playing. Later we will discuss in more detail the value of identifying those particular sights, sounds and feelings which we associate with success.

The Performance Loop

Think about the process of generating performance as a closed loop. Both external and internal stimuli play a part in determining our brain's interpretation of a situation and therefore our physical response to it (see diagram below). This loop starts with the external event, or action, that we perceive through our senses—i.e., our sight, sound and touch. That is interpreted by our brain; and the sensory experience, together with the interpretation, is what is called *perception*. Our brain then initiates a response to its interpretation—i.e., we react. We then experience our reaction through our senses, and start back through the loop all over again.

The Performance Loop

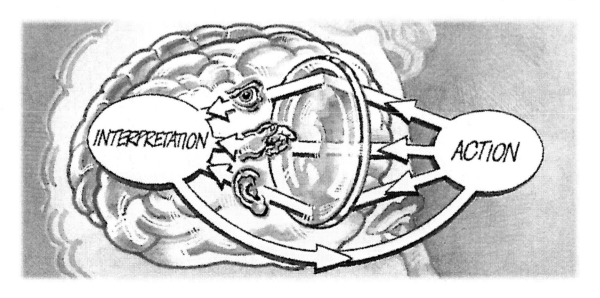

One Man's Threat...

When Ian Woosnam stands on the tee at the 17th at St. Andrews, he perceives it as a tough hole but a relatively comfortable first shot for him. He plays with a natural draw that enables him to deal more easily with the out-of-bounds down the righthand side. When you and I stand on this infamous Road Hole, we probably perceive a hole fraught with danger. It is the same hole, so who's right?

The infamous Road Hole at St. Andrews.

35

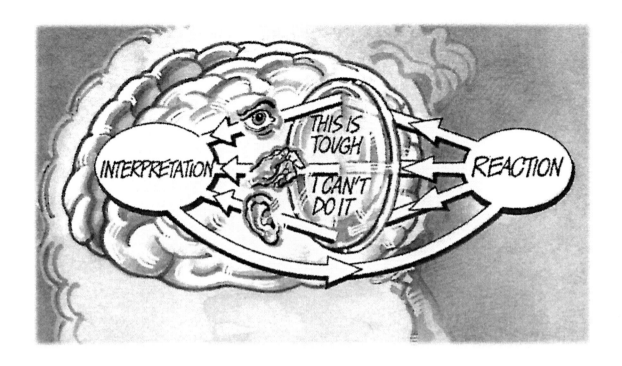

You will notice in the diagram that a lens is drawn in front of the brain. If our mind is quiet we hardly know this lens is there. The stimuli that come into our brains from our senses are "focused" by the lens so that we get a high-quality "image," and the result is that we get a high-quality reaction to this "image" or interpretation.

We all have beliefs (or paradigms) about ourselves, or about our golf, or both. These beliefs affect our perception, filtering the stimuli coming into our brain. Our beliefs are like dirt on the lens in the loop. When the stimuli we are sensing hit a belief, we cannot be sure that it will come straight through the lens and form an accurate image for our brain to interpret. From this inaccurate image we form an inaccurate interpretation—the mental state causes the physical response. The stronger the belief, the more dense the "dirt" on our lens is, and the more distorted the information coming through becomes.

Depending on how well we manage our mental state, these beliefs can work for us ("I can do it!") or against us ("I'm not good enough to do it"). But in golf, my experience is that more often than not our perception works against us. The beliefs we have tend to act as a filter, and they adversely affect the quality of the sensory information we need in order to control our actions and form rational conclusions.

Generally speaking, our learning and performance improve the more fully we experience what it is we are doing, and so one way to improve the efficiency of this loop is simply to clean our lens, i.e., change or remove our beliefs, so that our processing mechanism gets only the information it needs in order to form the right conclusions. That is what the focusing exercises we will come to later are designed to do.

When we hit a bad shot it means that we didn't swing correctly, that our actions were not the right ones. This does not happen spontaneously; it is caused by an inappropriate mental state which generated an inappropriate or inaccurate swing. Of course, the mental state might be triggered by some action. So now we have a chicken and egg situation—which comes first? As yet, I don't know. What matters to me is what can I do about it. And we are coming to that soon!

The Brain Drives Our Body

Our brain is like an engine room that drives our behavior, constantly receiving sensory stimuli, which we then sort and interpret according to our individual characteristics. These characteristics are different in all of us, and they reflect our own individual beliefs and our preferred way of sorting the information coming in. One thing we all have in common is that our physical performance is always related to our conclusions or interpretations, whatever they may be.

In other words, we always act in response to (or in a way that represents) the content of our thinking (or perception).

THINKING → ACTION.

Generally speaking, the better the quality with which we experience something, the more effective our learning and performance. Problems arise when our experience is clouded, either by our interpretation of the external stimuli (i.e., what we see, hear and feel), or by our interpretation of the internal stimuli (what our beliefs tell us).

ONE WORLD—TWO PERCEPTIONS

People can and do interpret the same information in the external world in many different ways. We have all been to different golf professionals for lessons and wondered why it is that they all say something different. Rarely are we given the same advice twice, yet they are all looking at the same swing—ours! The advice they give is genuine; however, they each have a different interpretation of what they see in our swing, and this prompts them to give different advice.

Give them a hammer, and all they see are nails...

When we consider buying a new car, once we have decided on the model we want to buy, that model is all we see on the road from then on.

Sometimes things aren't what they seem.

Although external reality might appear to be the same for everyone, it is our perception as an individual that establishes how this reality is interpreted. We each have a unique way of identifying and organizing information according to our past experiences, our current knowledge, and our future expectations. An event is therefore not only perceived, but also interpreted, in accordance with our moods, our feelings, the memories which that event evokes, the thoughts it triggers, and the hopes and fears it may cause. These factors all contribute to our mental condition and therefore affect our action.

THREATS AND OPPORTUNITIES

Let's explore in more detail the notion that it is our thinking, or mental state, that drives our performance.

When I'm working with a group of mixed-ability golfers, I sometimes ask the experienced players to explain to the beginners the basics of the game in terms of what they need to do to swing a golf club. They usually give some form of the following in reply:

"Hold the club with your right hand below your left..."

"Make sure that the 'V' that is formed between the thumb and index finger of each hand points up toward your right shoulder as you hold the club..."

"Stand with your feet comfortably apart, and place the ball somewhere between the middle of your stance and your left heel..."

"Make sure that the clubface is square to the ball at address..."

"Bend from the hips and flex your knees..."

"Take the club back smoothly, keeping your left arm reasonably straight…"

"Keep your head still..."

"Keep the club on the correct plane..."

I then ask the beginners in the group what this all sounds like to them. "Difficult" is the usual reply.

When we perceive something as being difficult, our usual response is to try harder to do that thing—here, it is swinging the golf club. When we try harder, we tighten our muscles, and that makes it more difficult to coordinate, so we are more likely to make an error. And when we make an error we say to ourselves, "That was difficult. I'd better try even harder." We get caught in a vicious circle.

... the green can seem like a postage stamp.
The Emirates Course in Dubai

39

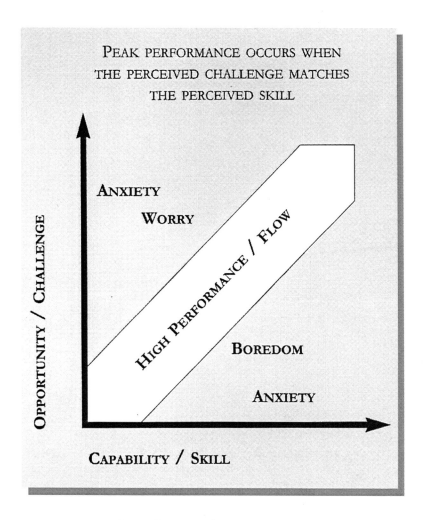

PEAK PERFORMANCE OCCURS WHEN
THE PERCEIVED CHALLENGE MATCHES
THE PERCEIVED SKILL

OPPORTUNITY / CHALLENGE

ANXIETY

WORRY

HIGH PERFORMANCE / FLOW

BOREDOM

ANXIETY

CAPABILITY / SKILL

Walking the Plank

Imagine walking along a four-inch wide plank laid out across the floor. We would have very little trouble doing this. Now imagine what it would be like to walk this same plank when it is five feet off the ground. Now we would be much more careful, hesitant and tight with every step we made. It is the same task, but we perceive it in very different ways, and our actions in response to our perception create very different results.

We perceive the challenge confronting us as too great for the skills we think we have. This induces worry and then anxiety (see diagram above), and in this condition our mental state is not conducive to creating our best performances or the learning of new skills.

I then reverse the process and ask the beginners to tell the experienced golfers what to do, and the task they set is usually very simple. Whatever the beginners tell the pros, the pros respond by saying, "That's too easy. It would be boring." They now perceive the skill they possess as being much greater than the challenge they face. The consequences of their trying to practice those instructions also show up in the diagram.

We can see from this diagram that if we keep the challenge facing us in balance with the skill we have, we will much more likely achieve the flow or optimum mental state. (The exercises later in this book are designed to do just that.)

(opposite) The balance of challenge and skill—in action.

41

*Phil Mickelson demonstrates
a positive mental attitude
winning the 2004 Masters.*

MENTAL STATE AND PEAK PERFORMANCE

In trying to understand what influences those rare moments of peak performance, sports psychologist James Loehr studied over 200 athletes. He discovered that their highest levels of performance occurred most often when they had a high level of energy, coupled with a positive mental attitude (see diagram below). On the basis of his research, Loehr concluded that the ideal mental condition for peak performance is one that features a calm mind, relaxed muscles and focused attention. In this state we say to ourselves, "I can do it." We believe that the skill we think we have is in balance with the challenge we are facing.

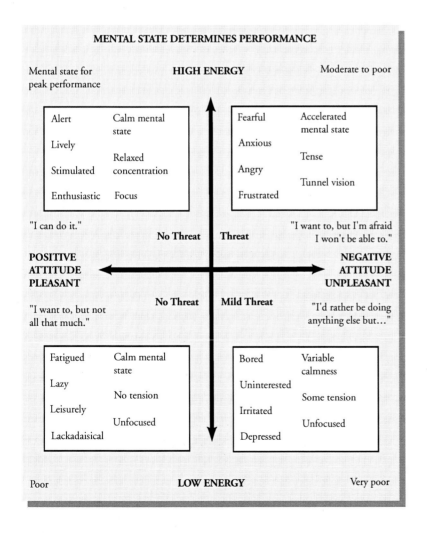

Our perception affects our performance —in anything.

For many people (especially me), making a speech in front of an audience is a nerve-racking experience. We are often anxious, particularly when we doubt our ability to perform the task well. These feelings are usually accompanied by physical reactions. Our throat feels "tight," and our mouth gets dry. When we start to speak, the words come out in a strangled fashion due to the tension in our throats. Our minds become busy with thoughts about what the audience will think of us, and it becomes difficult to organize in our mind what we want to say. The words come out jumbled, and we are hesitant. We see the audience begin to fidget, and one or two even start to talk among themselves. They fold their arms and we decide they are not impressed with what we have to say. So we try harder and tighten even more. This causes our voices to crack even more. The audience, sensing this, appears even more uncomfortable.

We have the vicious circle of belief, action based on belief, and perceived reaction of audience reinforcing our belief.

Loehr found that when people are negative in their attitude but high in energy, they are much less likely to achieve peak performance. In this situation we are inclined to say to ourselves, "I want to, but I'm afraid I won't be able to do it" (see diagram previous page).

We feel threatened because the challenge we think we face appears to be much greater than the skill we think we have. Although there is plenty of the high energy for the performance, it can easily result in burnout.

Loehr also found that when people are both negative in their attitude and low in energy, they are much less likely to achieve peak performance.

He established that the optimum mental attitude preceded high performance—not the other way around.

In other words, the mental state came before and facilitated the performance. We all recognize that if we play well, our energy goes up and we feel good. But it is much easier to raise the energy and create focus in order to play better than it is to play better in order to feel good. That, of course, is what this book is about.

THE GOLFER'S NIGHTMARE—TRYING TOO HARD

Trying too hard is such a common phenomenon in golf that it's worth spending a little more time on it.

We are taught from birth that we must try as hard as we can to achieve our goals, and on the whole this is very commendable. But try the arm-bending exercise shown on the opposite page. Here, the harder you tried, the worse your performance. When you seemingly tried less hard, it became much easier to keep your arm straight.

We have probably all experienced this phenomenon at work in our golf. We are out on the practice range with a driver, trying to hit the ball as far as we can—let's say 250 yards. And although we've been trying very hard to hit the ball a long way, our best effort has only just crossed the 200-yard marker. There are only six balls left, so we give up. We decide to relax and just enjoy hitting them; we're not trying to hit them a long way or think very much about what we're doing technically. We're simply having fun. And what happens? Our muscles relax, we coordinate our swing much better, and we generate the clubhead speed that's necessary to hit the ball a long way. Suddenly we realize that we've just hit one past the 250-yard marker, and we say to ourselves, "That's it. I've got it. I'll try to do that again." And as soon as we say that to ourselves, we're right back where we started. Our mental state is back in the "trying too hard" mode, our muscles tighten, and our ability to create clubhead speed is lost.

Hold one arm straight out in front of you. Ask a friend to put one hand in the crook of your elbow and the other hand under your wrist and then to try to bend your arm at the elbow (1). (Make sure the friend bends it with, not against, the joint!) Your job is to resist as hard as you can without moving. Both of you need to gauge how much effort you need to use in order to do your respective tasks.

Then ask your friend to do exactly the same again. This time imagine that you have a beam of light (like a laser beam) coming out of your fingers. Imagine the beam hitting the wall, or whatever it is pointing at, and imagine smoke coming out of the hole it is burning, with smoke and flames, etc. Ignore what your partner is doing as he tries to bend your arm again (2).

In figure (1) you are in the mental state of trying hard, but you are using the wrong muscles, and it will be hard work to keep your arm from bending. But when you keep your mind fully focused on the light beam, as in figure (2), you change your mental state to one of focused attention, and it becomes easier to keep your arm straight and harder for your partner to bend it.

Trying hard needs to be directed in the right area to be really effective in what we're doing technically.

EXPERIENCE, LEARNING AND PERFORMANCE

In his work on the *Inner Game of Golf,* Timothy Gallwey describes a relationship between experience, learning and performance that sparked some investigation on my part.

I had always wondered why it was that beginners seemed to improve very quickly during their first few months, but then reached a plateau in their progress. As I began to do more work in golf I noticed a pattern emerging, one that seemed to reflect the relationship that Gallwey had identified between experience, learning and performance.

It would appear to me that people take up golf for a number of different reasons, including

- to meet the challenge of the game.
- to get exercise.
- to experience the peace and quiet.
- to be with family or friends.
- to be away from family or friends.
- to prove themselves.

Whatever our reason, we usually derive some form of enjoyment from the game. As beginners, we have few expectations of playing well. In other words, we have a very easy-going and relaxed attitude—one similar to the peak performance state discussed earlier—and this in turn causes our performance to rise very rapidly.

Then other people begin to notice our improvement and say things like, "Aren't you doing well. You've improved tremendously..." And naturally we enjoy all the praise and attention. It satisfies our ego and obviously means that we are doing something right.

We begin to look forward to the compliments and the flattering remarks about our performance, and slowly (and without realizing it) our attention shifts away from simply playing for enjoyment to trying to ensure that we do not play any worse than before. In other words, our attention becomes caught up in our performance, on trying to maintain a standard rather than experiencing what we were doing. And our performance and learning drop dramatically as a result (see diagram, opposite). Of course we eventually pass through this stage, and start improving again.

The next time I saw this happen was with golfers who had just turned professional. Again, the emphasis changed from experiencing and learning to performance. The justification this time is "Now it is serious. My living depends on it." They are right, of course. Their living does depend on it, but approaching the game with this attitude sends the wrong stimuli into the performance loop, and as a result we get the wrong output. Experience is what teaches us how to do what we want to do, or know we should do.

H.E.L.P.

This is an acronym I use in training coaches which may be just as relevant to us as players. It represents:

Help intensify
Experience to increase
Learning and raise
Performance

In the performance loop, our interpretation is based on what we experience, and this experience is based on a combination of our beliefs and the sensory input from the external world. Remember, what we experience are the external stimuli filtered through our beliefs. Our problem is that often the stimuli that eventually get

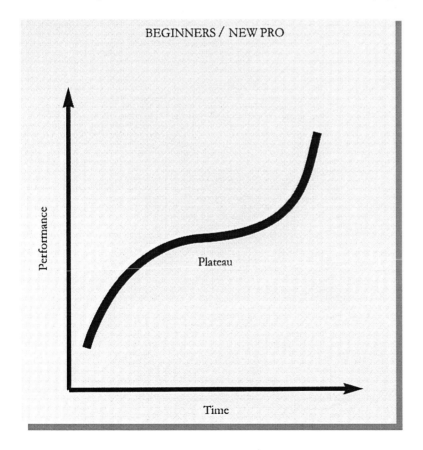

through our beliefs represent an inaccurate picture of the external world. But they are the stimuli we respond to, the ones that drive our behavior and therefore our performance.

The more we can intensify our experience of events, or the more we are aware of what we are doing, the more we learn (i.e., change our behavior), and the better our performance becomes. It goes in that order. This does not mean that we must at all times consciously know everything about what we are doing. As we discovered with the pendulum and arm-bending experiments, our subconscious is a very powerful tool if we feed it the right information. Input the right stimuli and you get the right output. Input the wrong stimuli and you get the wrong output. It's a simple equation. As they say in computing, garbage in = garbage out.

The trick is to increase your understanding of what stimuli to feed into the performance loop, and how to feed these in so that you get the output or performance you want.

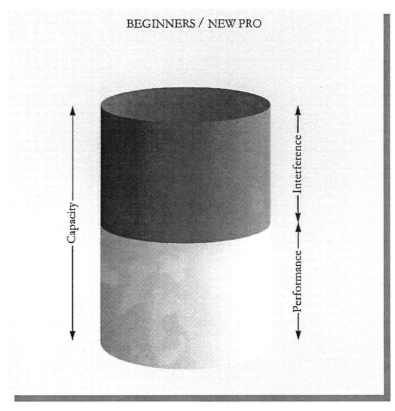

Performance = Capacity - Interference

Assumptions. Sit down with your eyes closed and raise your arms out in front of you so that one points upwards at 45 degrees and one points downward at 45 degrees. Hold this for 30 seconds and then put both arms horizontally out in front of you parallel with the ground without opening your eyes. As soon as you have that done, open your eyes and see what you have done.

MENTAL INTERFERENCE

Timothy Gallwey coined the phrase "mental interference" in his inner game books. He suggests that a player's performance at any given moment is equal to his capacity to perform (i.e., his current level of ability) less the interference present (i.e., the things that distract his attention). See the diagram on page 48. This interference can be either external or internal. In golf, external interferences would include the weather, the condition of the course, the presence of spectators, or even the performance of the opponent. Internal interferences, on the other hand, are the distractions already firmly implanted in our mind, a constant stream of internal chatter. Internal interference is often the more powerful, and is caused by

- the ego (expectations, perfectionism, self-consciousness)
- lack of self-confidence, fear, or self-condemnation
- false assumptions

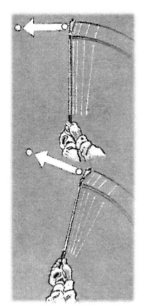

Making assumptions.

Fear can be a real dilemma for the golfer. At its worst, it manifests itself in what are called the *yips*—a jerky, erratic movement that can send the ball in all directions. Our perception of the threat facing us is so frightening that it evokes what psychologists call the "flight or fight" response. Yipping usually refers to a golfer's putting stroke, but it is possible to identify the same symptoms in any part of the game (fear of bunkers, chipping, pitching, etc.)

Imagine getting ready to hit a 3-foot putt to win the monthly medal or a check for $100,000 (it's not the amount that matters here, it's our perception of the challenge we face). If we perceive the challenge as being way too much for our skill—which a 3-foot putt to someone who has the yips would be—we get ready for action that would deal with a huge threat.

Given the performance loop, we will respond to our interpretation according to our experience of the events, and the way in which we experienced the stimuli would tell us that we are in danger. Under this kind of threat our bodies automatically pump more blood into the large muscles and put more adrenaline into our system to get us ready to either fight the threat or run from it. However, we don't want this kind of response in golf, particularly when we are putting, because it causes large, powerful, but inappropriate muscle movements, and we need small fine movements to putt accurately.

Making assumptions about where our body is in space is a frequent cause of trouble in golf (as shown in the exercise opposite). If we are unable to tell whether our hands are in one position or another, we are unlikely to be able to sense what position the clubhead is in either. If we think the clubhead is in position A, and it is actually in position B, we have a problem—and it gets worse.

Let me give you an example. Imagine that we hit a ball and it flies off to the right. Now we already know what causes this because we've read about it, and the pro has confirmed that in our case one of the problems is the position of our hands at impact. So we consciously try to release our hands a little more forcefully through impact to get the clubface into the correct position to strike the ball. But the problem is not that we don't know what to do, it's that we can't tell with any accuracy where our club face is in the first place—so how can we possibly expect to correct it? The trick is to increase our awareness of where the clubface actually is by experiencing it more fully.

BELIEFS

A crucial element in feeding the wrong stimuli into our performance loop is our beliefs. Beliefs are hard to define and recognize, yet they have a very powerful effect on our performance. Beliefs are things we think about the actual events that happen. They may or may not be accurate. They are not the events themselves.

Examples of the beliefs that affect our performance in golf are "I can't play out of sand." "I always slice." "They are better than I am." "My clubs aren't right." "I never have been very coordinated."

Our beliefs act as filters to the information provided by our senses. They screen the information in a way that causes us to interpret the stimuli and react in a way that we don't really want. Let's take a typical example. I'd like you to meet Steven Slicer!

Steven begins his round fairly happy with his form, but on the 1st tee he carves his ball away into the rough beside the fairway. He watches the flight of the ball, and then says to himself, "I sliced that one." He continues to play, and minutes later does the same thing at the 3rd. This time he observes the slice, and then says, "I am slicing today." At the 6th he carves another one way into the trees on the right, and this time declares, "I have a slice today." A little further into the round and our hero hits another terrible slice at the 14th, and this time concludes, "I am a slicer." Then, on the 15th, he misses a short putt and says, "I am no good at this game."

Losing at squash the next day provokes the thought, "I am not very good at sports," and when things don't go right at work, "I am not a good person."

And so Steven Slicer gets caught up in the performance loop in a very destructive way. It starts when he observes a slice. When he sees the second one go that way, he decides he may have a slice. The next one reinforces his belief that he has this problem, and now he's looking for the thing he fears most—another slice! This causes him to try not to slice, which causes tension, locking the club face and causing even more slice. When it happens again, he turns to his partners and celebrates, "That's me, you see. I told you I always slice the ball."

His belief becomes so strong that on the rare occasions when he does hit the ball straight he just says to himself (and others), "Oh, that's just lucky. I can't really do that." In this way he can ignore the evidence that contradicts his belief that he is a slicer. And the more he tries to prevent his slice, the worse it inevitably gets.

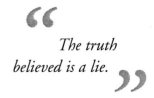

The truth believed is a lie.

Anon

KEY POINTS — CHAPTER THREE

- Mental skills allow us to perform our physical skills.

- Understanding something doesn't mean that we can do it.

- People have an innate ability to learn.

- Experiencing what we are doing helps us learn and perform.

- Managing our perception is the key to experiencing.

- Interference blocks our perception of the world.

- We can harness this ability to learn by understanding brain dominance and sensory modes.

Two Brains, Three Senses—More About How We Work

Those of us who studied human biology in school will remember being taught that the brain has two hemispheres, the left hemisphere and the right hemisphere. We may have been taught that these different hemispheres control different aspects of our functioning as human beings. What I certainly wasn't taught was how significant these hemispheres are to our golf.

I was also taught that I have five senses. What we have learned since is that three of these senses play a vital role in our golf in terms of how we conceptualize or think about our golf (or anything, for that matter) and how we perceive and act in the external world.

First, let's look at our two hemispheres or two brains.

RIGHT AND LEFT BRAINS?

There are three important things to note when we talk about the different halves of the brain:

1. They control different functions in us.
2. A lot of us tend to lean toward being more left- or more right-brained in our approach to golf and life generally.
3. Golf as an activity has some elements that demand the use of our left hemisphere, and other elements that demand more use of our right hemisphere.

Let me explain some more by comparing the differences between right-brain dominant people—described as "right-brainers"—and left-brain dominant people—or "left-brainers."

Left-brainers are logical, timely, reliable, neat, realistic and analytical. They can be critical, they like things to be well planned and

organized. They thrive on routine, will practice for hours, and generally want to understand thoroughly before doing.

Right-brainers are imaginative and impetuous, take risks and break rules. They are holistic, good at conceptualizing, intuitive, creative and sensitive. They are curious, like surprises, relate well to feel (are kinesthetic), and enjoy movement.

Of course no one is totally right-brained or totally left-brained, but most of us tend to be more one way or the other. That makes it easier for us to learn or do the things that demand the use of the dominant half of our brain, and harder for us to learn or do the things that demand the use of the non-dominant half of our brain.

Bearing in mind the above, here is how we run into difficulties. Imagine that I tend to be more left-brained in my approach to life. I will tend to apply my left-brained approach to the whole of my golf, and I will perform well the elements of golf that demand the functions of my left brain. However, the elements that demand the use of my right brain will suffer, because I still try to apply my preferred left-brain mode of thinking. It's a bit like trying to screw in a normal slotted screw with a Phillips screwdriver. It's the wrong tool for the job, and it makes life very difficult.

LEFT OR RIGHT-BRAINED GOLF

Now think about golf. As an activity it has two distinct phases. The first phase is what I call the pre-swing, and it involves our activity before we hit the ball. It contains our arriving at the ball, analyzing the situation we are faced with, working out the shot we need to make, assessing whether or not we have the skill to execute it, selecting a club for the job and beginning our routine, which would probably include carefully lining up.

The second phase comes once we have finished our pre-swing routine. This is the moment when we hit the ball. It is the time when we need to stop thinking and allow the pre-swing work we have been doing to have its effect. It is when we need to experience what we are actually doing. We have pointed our brains in the right direction and now we let our bodies get on with it.

If we refer back to the characteristics of left- and right-brained thinking, it's easy to see that our left brain is best suited to the first phase (pre-swing), while the right brain is best suited to the activities of the second phase (playing). The left brain is good at taking care of the analysis and decision making; the right brain is good at acting on that analysis and decision.

The left brain at work.

In my experience the dilemma for the majority of us is that we tend to take the left-brained approach into the right-brained orientated activities. We are still analyzing and instructing ourselves in the moments when we need to be just doing, and experiencing what we are doing. The problem for many people is that trusting the right brain to take care of the physical action without conscious guidance can feel like taking a risk—that we have less control and that we are unsure what will happen next.

A significant number of us will also do the reverse—I'm one of them. Being right-brain dominant, I prefer to do something quite quickly before analyzing it. So when I play golf I want to get on and hit the ball without analyzing the situation properly and without going through a proper pre-shot routine.

It is important to realize that none of this is good or bad, or right or wrong. It is just how we are as human beings, and the better we understand our predispositions, the better we can use them in our favor. By identifying which is the dominant half of our brain, we can work on developing the skills of our non-dominant half by practicing activities that demand those skills. In my case, being a right-brained dominant thinker, I would improve my performance if I introduced a

The right brain at work.

little more left-brain discipline into my game, and developed a specific pre-shot routine that helped me to eliminate elementary errors. A left-brainer, on the other hand, might learn to reduce the analysis and self-instruction, and let his subconscious get on with hitting the ball. The various focusing exercises that we will come to later are designed to eliminate this sort of internal interference (and can be applied both in practice and out on the course).

THE THREE SENSES—SEEING, FEELING AND HEARING

We said earlier that the way we know there is a world out there is through our senses, and that because there was not very much smelling and tasting to do in golf, the major senses that tell us about our golfing world are seeing, feeling and hearing. We experience, interpret and act on the stimuli that are relayed through our senses. These stimuli come to us in varying combinations of visual (seeing) data, kinesthetic (feeling) data and auditory (hearing) data.

When we think about our golf, we think in terms of visual, kinesthetic and auditory concepts. The concept in our mind may be visual—we may associate with, or form pictures in our mind about, whatever we are thinking about. It may be kinesthetic—we may associate with or form feelings in our mind about what we are thinking about.

It may also be auditory—we may associate with or form sounds about what we are thinking about. Most of us will conceptualize using various amounts of all three.

It seems that we have the same mechanism at work whether we are sensing the outside world or our own internal world. We create our sense of meaning of the world by combining the input from these three senses.

However, we also have a specific sense that dominates our consciousness in telling us about the world, whether that world is our internal one or the external one. Just as we have a dominant right or left hemisphere in our brain, we have dominant sensory ways of thinking in each of these hemispheres. Using our dominant sensory mode can be as important as using the appropriate side of the brain for the right task in golf when we come to determining the keys to peak performance.

It is much easier for us to understand things that are described in our dominant mode. Some of us respond much more readily to visual language and communication. For example, we "see the swing," or "get the picture." Some "grasp the idea" or "get a feel for it," while others "hear what you mean" or "get the rhythm" of the swing. Understanding which is our dominant mode (we also have secondary modes) can help speed up our learning process, make it easier to concentrate, and help us be more reliable under pressure. The key to high performance and accelerated learning is to manage the stimuli coming into the performance loop; and understanding our dominant modes can help us do that.

The three senses: seeing, feeling and hearing.

THE MANAGEMENT OF PERCEPTION

So what? So we have a dominant side to our brains. So we have a preferred sensory mode. What do we do with all this?

Remember, it is our brain that drives or causes our action, and so it follows that the better we drive our brain, the better it will drive that action. And the brain is a superb mechanism. With it, we learned how to walk and talk long before we were able to tell ourselves what and how to walk and talk—or swing a golf club. So, given the performance loop, we potentially have two places that we can exert some influence over things. One is our perception of the external world, and the other is our perception of our internal world, both of which go to make up our experience of the world as a whole. As we get into the exercises, I will suggest some that help with one or the other, and some that work with both.

First, let's begin to think about which are our dominant modes. Read through these descriptions and decide which one is closer to you. We are not aiming to be statistically or psychologically accurate here, just to provide some food for thought.

RIGHT-BRAIN DOMINANT

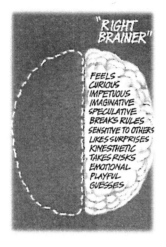

When I play, I

Like to imagine/create new shots.

Am sometimes reckless in my choice of shot.

Guess the yardage.

Hit the ball in unconventional ways (when others think it's unnecessary).

Like to play the bold shot.

Enjoy new courses and playing partners.

Like to have fun when playing.

Can tell when something is bothering other people and try to change it.

Get the feel of things.

Get highs and lows in response to how well I am doing.

Am curious about other ways to achieve the end result.

LEFT-BRAIN DOMINANT

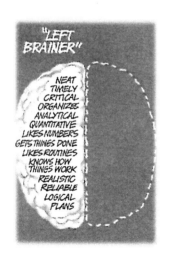

When I play, I

Like to analyze every swing I make, especially if it goes wrong.

Want logical explanations for everything I do.

Always arrive to play on time.

Do what I say I will.

Like routines.

Am critical of myself (and others) if things are not right.

Try to be realistic with my goals.

Prefer practice that can be measured, quantified and analyzed.

Like to understand why I do things.

Always dress neatly.

Plan how I will play a hole.

Organize my playing, practice and social schedule.

Of course no one is totally one or the other of these, but most of us lean one way or another in our preferences. Some of us will lean only slightly one way. Others will be closer to one of the two extremes. If we are more right-brained in our preferences, then the pre-swing phase is where we can make a significant gain. If we are more left-brained in our preferences, then we have probably analyzed our swing to death already. We will need to learn to let go of our thinking about the right way to do things while we make our swing.

SENSORY MODES

Learning which are our dominant modes takes time and is easier for some people to do than others. Some clues as to which sense might be our dominant one are set out below.

If our dominant sensory mode is visual, we tend to notice or remember

- brightness or intensity
- color
- size
- location in space
- shape
- movement

We use words like "see," "perspective," "point of view." We talk faster than others, and wear bright, neat clothing. We learn easily from visual aids, walk quite quickly, watch television to relax, form first impressions of people and remember things by what they look like.

If our dominant mode is kinesthetic, we tend to notice or remember

- bodily sensations
- emotions
- movement
- temperature
- pressure
- humidity
- texture
- rhythm
- balance

We use words like "feel," "grasp," "get the hang of." We have slower, deeper voices and dress casually and comfortably. We learn more easily from doing, we walk slowly, slouch in a chair to relax and respond to feelings—we are good empathizers.

If our dominant sensory mode is auditory, we tend to notice or remember these aspects of what we hear:

- pitch
- tone
- clarity
- duration
- tempo
- rhythm
- loudness
- location in space

We use words like "hear," and phrases like "that rings a bell," or "the noise in my system." We have rhythmic voices and learn better from people with good voices. We walk with a distinct rhythm, listen to music to relax, and are comfortable being on our own.

Some of you will recognize quite quickly which of these apply most to you, while others will find it much more difficult. There is no right preference, no dominant mode that will make you a better golfer. And no, you are not a hopeless case if you cannot immediately identify your dominant modes—it takes practice.

However, if there is a secret in golf, it lies in learning to manage our sensory modes and preferences in ways that produce the results we want. At some time or another we have all played well or pulled off a spectacular shot, and when we did, the various facets of our mental state jelled. What we need to do is identify what characterized this mental state, and look at ways to induce it more often.

In the next chapter we will identify some ways to uncover our preferences and begin to manage our brains in ways that help us produce more of what we want more of the time.

DISCOMFORT

In my experience, one of the biggest problems that face us when we want to improve is that we don't like to change. Many of us prefer to remain within our "comfort" zone as we go about our learning, but doing this makes progress a very slow process. If we want to improve, we must he prepared to do something differently—to change what we do—and that means moving into our "stretch zone" (see skiing example). But change, for many of us, is an uncomfortable process, and to avoid this discomfort we often go back to doing what we are used to— old habits die hard. And not surprisingly, we get the same old results. We always get the results of our actions. Always!

To encourage us to be willing to approach things differently, here is one more way to think about the learning process. It is not the truth. No model is. But it may simplify and therefore help us to

Comfort Zones

A useful model of mental states comes from skiing, where skiers talk about comfort, stretch and panic zones. In comfort zones, boredom eventually sets in—we think our skill is greater than the challenge. In panic, there is so much interference that it can paralyze us—we think the challenge is so much greater than our skill that it has become a threat. Most improvement takes place in the stretch zone, where the challenge is in proportion to our skill.

understand how our performance happens. You will notice a process that goes on subconsciously, which I have called "integration" and "execution." We don't know it is happening, because it is subconscious, but it happens nonetheless.

We always like to know what we are doing. Our egos like to be in charge, so much so that many of us find it very difficult just to allow this subconscious process to work. We always want to be consciously changing something—despite all the evidence that when we played at our best or learned at our fastest, we were less consciously involved in the doing. It was just happening. Think about it.

When we play well, don't we go back to the clubhouse and say, "I don't know how it happened but it just clicked today. I didn't think about it, I just did it"! Our integrator and executor are doing a great job of learning and performing for us. When we play badly, we are often busy thinking about what we are doing and trying to change things. We don't want to trust our subconscious to take control, or, as Timothy Gallwey describes it, "trust and let go." The idea of allowing our subconscious to do things for us can become a threat and produce the effects we have discussed before, yet we need to learn to use it.

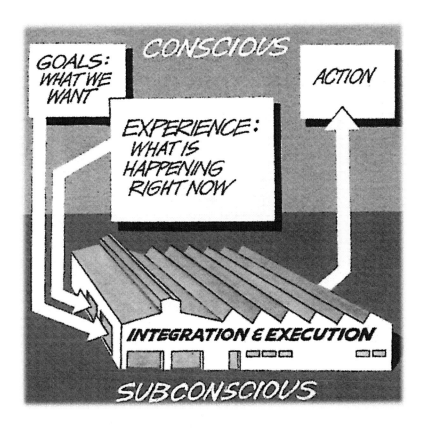

How we learn ... Another way to think about it.

Most of what we experience is actually processed subconsciously. The trick is to manage the conscious portion of our experience so that it points the subconscious in the right direction. My hope is that we now have some understanding of how our brain drives our body. If this has seemed incomplete in any way, that's because our understanding of this field is. We have advanced a long way, yet we are still in our infancy in psychology compared with swing technique.

So now let's turn our attention to some ways to apply these theories practically to our golf. Once more, the principle is that our brain drives our body, and our perception drives our brain. When we manage what we perceive by managing the stimuli, then we have our best chance of reaching peak performance.

"Making that walk up 18, through the lengthening shadows on a sun-splashed day, having brought a killer course to its knees in a tournament everyone thirsts to win, Stephen Ames stopped once, managed a deep breath, and took the whole scene in.

...Ames hit 72 percent of the greens, 75 percent of the fairways. The man was so good, so in control, so impenetrable, that a tournament annually cloaked in drama became a one-man soapbox."

-George Johnson, Calgary Herald

(Opposite: Stephen Ames at the 2006 Players Championship)

KEY POINTS — CHAPTER FOUR

- Goals should be SMART—specific, measurable, achievable, relevant, and time-phased.

- We should use both performance and learning goals.

- Goals are more powerful when described in sensory terms.

The Way Forward

Now that we have explored some of the basics about how we generate performance, we can begin to apply some of the theory practically. To help us perform at our peak, our brains need a map to follow—just as a computer needs a program to follow. The key elements of this map are these:

- It enables us to identify the direction we want to go, i.e., goal-setting.
- It is structured in such a way that we are able to recognize when we reach our goal, using language that our brain understands.
- It provides us with a plan of specifically what we will do (the tools or exercises) and how we will do it (practice), and gives us a way to recognize or reward ourselves for doing things that produce the desired results.

So let's first talk about goal setting.

GOAL SETTING

Goals are what give our brains a direction to go in. Most of us use them to one degree or another in our lives, career development, or hobbies. We often hear about successful people having very clear objectives. But just saying "I want to get better at golf" or "I want to win a tournament," as many people do, doesn't give your brain much to go on. It is like saying "I want to travel" to our travel agent. To be able to help, she would need to know where we want to go and how we want to get there. So do our brains!

WHERE AM I RIGHT NOW?

To help us set useful goals we need to know where we are starting from—where we are right now. Imagine trying to get to Chicago from Miami. We have a map that shows us where Chicago is but does not show Miami. It makes it very hard to know what the next step should be to get to Chicago.

SELF ASSESSMENT GRID

On the left list the skills and qualities that you believe are essential to your becoming a better golfer. Score yourself from 1 to 10 against each item. 10 means you are as strong as you think you can be on that particular item; 1 means you think you are very weak on that particular item.

If you are interested in a more neutral opinion of your skills, you might ask other people who know you and your skills to fill out a column for you.

SKILL QUALITIES	OTHER	OTHER	OTHER	AV.	SELF
Long Game	8	8	7	7.7	6
Fitness	4	5	3	4	(4)
Short Game	6	7	7	6.7	8
Practice	2	3	4	(3	6)
Mental Skills	7	6	6	6.3	(5)
Long Game	9	10	9	9.3	9

REMEMBER, THIS IS NOT THE TRUTH!

In the grid opposite you will see an exercise I use to help golfers think through the current status of their golf game so that they have a better idea where they are starting from. I ask people to think of the skills and qualities that are essential to become a good golfer and list them down the left column (driving, bunker play, physical fitness, concentration etc.) Then I ask them to rate themselves from 1 to 10 on each item, where 1 means that they are very weak on that item, and 10 means that they are as strong as they think they could be. I also invite them to ask other people who are familiar with their game and whose opinions they trust to fill in a rating for them, and then take the average of those scores.

We then look at the two sets of data. One is the self-score they gave. This often shows up gaps in their awareness—they say, "I did not realize it until I thought about it...." The other is a way of injecting some neutral opinion into their thinking as a check on the accuracy of their own assessment. When there is a gap of 2 or more (plus or minus) between the self-score and the other score, it warrants some extra attention as to why.

Both of these pieces of data point to where some change might be useful, and setting goals is the first step in this change process.

The three aspects of goal setting are

- Making the goals SMART.
- The difference between learning and performance goals.
- Putting the goals into the language of our brain.

SMART GOALS

We can and will talk about goals in several different ways, but in each of these ways, to make them useful we need to make them SMART. This stands for

Specific
Measurable
Achievable
Relevant
Time-phased

Specific: Goals need to be specific so that we can easily identify what they are and where they will lead us. Saying "I want to be a better golfer" is so vague that no matter what we do, we can (and usually do) say to ourselves, "Yes, I am improving, but I'm still not good enough." In other words, we aren't yet perfect. We need to specify how we will recognize that we are a better golfer. Here are a few examples:

Yes, but...

In teaching, most pros have run into the "yes but" syndrome. In beginners, it manifests itself when students say that they want to be a better golfer. The pro works with them for half an hour, and at the end of that time they can hit the ball up in the air. Significant progress! The pro asks, "How are we doing?" The student replies, "Yes, it's OK, but it doesn't go very far, does it?" So the pro works for another half hour with the student, and the ball goes much farther.

"How are we doing now?"

"Yes it's going farther, but it's not very straight, is it...?"

And so it goes on. No matter what happens, the student always says "Yes, but..." because his goals were not set accurately at the outset.

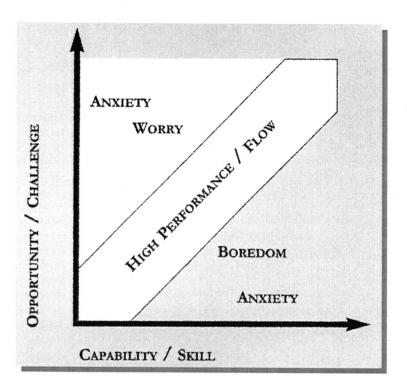

1. "I want to eliminate my slice. In practice, I want to be able to drive 5 out of 10 balls into an imaginary fairway without slicing, and 3 out of 10 when I am on the golf course."

2. "I want to be able to hit 9 out of 10 shots with a full body turn."

Measurable: This is so that we know when we have attained them. Unless we can measure our performance against the goal we are aiming for, we will never know whether we have attained it, which means we never get to feel successful. So, building on the second example above,

1. "I want to be able to hit 9 out of 10 shots with a full-body turn, which to me means getting my hips and shoulders rotated another quarter-turn."

Now we have something tangible to measure, so that we can recognize any change in our turn, using video and expert observation.

Achievable: Our goals need to be achievable (and challenging) so that they don't become boring or threatening. We have to believe that the goal is achievable, or it will create interference for us. As Csikszentmihayli and Loehr found out, if we think that the goal or challenge is too difficult for our level of skill, it will be threatening to us and produce worry, anxiety, tense muscles and poor performance (see diagram opposite), e.g.,

1. "In practice, I want to be able to drive 5 out of 10 balls without slicing and 3 out of 10 when I am on the golf course. I have only been able to hit 1 shot in 10 without slicing so far."

This implies a 500 percent improvement...

2. "I want to be able to hit 9 out of 10 shots with a full-body turn. I have never done it so far."

An infinite percentage improvement!

If we believe the goal doesn't challenge our level of skill, then it will produce boredom and eventually anxiety, low energy levels and loss of focus (see diagram below), e.g.,

1. "In practice, I want to be able to drive 5 out of 10 balls without slicing and 3 out of 10 when I am on the golf course. I can do 4 out of 10 in practice already."
2. "I want to be able to hit 9 out of 10 shots with a full-body turn. I can do 8 out of 10 already."

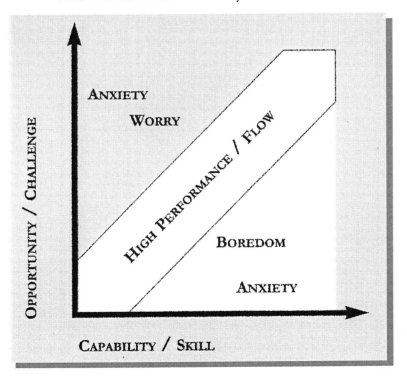

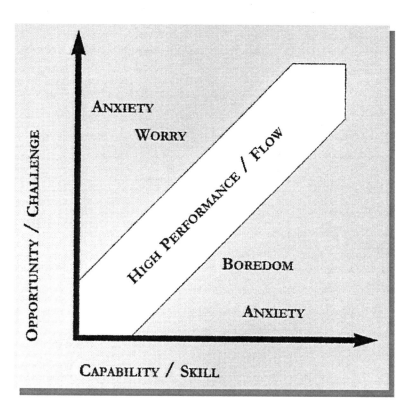

There is not much challenge in either case, so neither of these goals generates much enthusiasm or energy.

When we think our goal is achievable but know we will have to stretch for it, then we are more likely to get a quiet mind, relaxed muscles, and focused attention—the flow state (see diagram above), e.g.,

1. "In practice, I want to be able to drive 5 out of 10 balls without slicing and 3 out of 10 when I am on the golf course. Currently I think I can do 3 on the range and 2 on the course."
2. "I want to be able to hit 9 out of 10 shots with a full-body turn. I can do 6 at the moment."

A 66 percent improvement in both examples. Challenging but not impossible!

Relevant: When a goal is not meaningful to us, then it becomes hard to muster the energy necessary to go after it. Goals imposed by other people, or those which we adopt because we have seen other people be successful with them, usually don't have enough relevance to excite us, e.g.,

1. "I want to be able to hit 9 out of 10 shots with a full-body turn. I can do 6 at the moment, but I'd rather try to improve my length off the tee." "I want to, but not all that much" is what's being said here. "The goal is not relevant to me right now."

Time-phased: When do we want to achieve the goal by? The time-phase we set will be an important factor in determining how achievable and relevant the goal is to us, e.g.,

1. "In practice, I want to be able to drive 5 out of 10 balls without slicing and 3 out of 10 when I am on the golf course by the end of this half-hour practice session. Currently I think I can do 3 on the range and 2 on the course.

The time-phase might make this unrealistic or not achievable.

2. "I want to be able to hit 9 out of 10 shots with a full-body turn by the end of the month. I can do 6 at the moment, and I practice 3 times a week."

Now we are getting the goal to be **SMART**.
We sometimes hear people talk of short-, medium-, and long-term goals. It can be useful to use all of them in golf, as long as they are SMART.

Intensive Practice—Vijay Singh

Was that SMART, Alan?

Making the goal SMART helped me stop the "yes buts" when playing the first hole at Whitchurch a few years ago. The lady pro I was playing with asked me what I wanted to achieve at this hole. I said, "Merely get the ball onto the green." It was a par 3 and about a 5-iron for me. The pro went first and topped the ball into the rough. Now I was really nervous! I placed my ball on the tee, reminded myself that the goal was to just get on the green and swung. I watched as the ball arched straight at the flag. It stopped about ten yards short. I turned to my partner, who was congratulating me on my shot, and said, "Yes, but if only I had taken a 4-iron I would have been inches from the hole!" She turned to me and asked, "What was your goal?" "Yes, but—" She interrupted, "What did you say your goal was?" She reminded me of my S.M.A.R.T. goal so that I could measure my success and feel more confident about the next shot instead of less confident because I hadn't done it perfectly!

Watch for big problems; they disguise big opportunities.

H. Jackson Brown, Jr.

Short-term goals extend from right now to, say, three months away. We set them in terms of a goal for our practice session today (holing 60 percent of six-foot putts), or a goal for some specific improvement by the end of that three-month period—or both. It means deciding specifically what we want to walk away from our practice session having achieved. If we have made our short-term goals SMART, they allow us to experience some immediate progress, and that helps to boost our energy level—so crucial for performance—and our confidence. If we give some careful thought to our practice session goals, we can experience a success every time we go out. And there is nothing like success to breed further success. The little wins that we accumulate in the short-term add up, and over a period of time they all contribute to the long-term "big win" and all help us develop the habit of being successful—the performance loop again.

Medium-term goals go from three months to two years. They give us significant checkpoints en route to our final destination. If our long-term goal is a handicap of 5, then a medium-term goal might be to get down to single figures within twelve months.

Long-term goals are anything that goes beyond two years. They are a way of expressing our vision or dreams more tangibly. They keep us inspired and energized to take action. The youngster wants to become a pro, the club golfer wants to break 80, etc.

LEARNING AND PERFORMANCE GOALS

Making any goal SMART makes a difference in how useful the goal can be. However, other facets of setting goals are worth considering.

Performance Goals

Many of us understand the importance of setting goals for ourselves, and when we set them, most of us tend to set performance goals, such as winning the club competition by June, or shooting below 90 within one year, or finishing in the top ten in a tour event by July. All these are examples of performance goals. But while they are important and necessary to us, they each have one problem in common. They can all be affected by forces outside our control, e.g., other players, or the weather.

Imagine our goal is winning the monthly medal by June. We play our best golf ever, walk in with a net 65, and deserve to win—and would have won any other medal that year. But someone else is also having a good day, and as a result has scored a net 64. Any other time, we would have achieved our goal, but now we walk away feeling dissatisfied because it seems as if we have failed. It's the same if we aim for a top ten finish. In fact, we have watched tour players seemingly do all they needed to do to make the Ryder Cup team, only to be beaten at the last minute by someone winning a big money tournament just before selection. They may do very little else all season, but if our goal was to be on the Ryder Cup team, then again we have failed. If we aim to break 90, the week we are on our best form may have the worst weather of the season. Yet again we have failed.

To make performance goals as effective as possible, we need to find ways to measure changes in our performance that are less dependent on external factors. Let's look at an example. Think of a tournament golfer new to the tour. He wants to win his first tournament. Whether the event is large or small does not matter—he just wants to get a win under his belt. He has come close to winning several times and is now beginning to lose heart. All he can perceive now is failure.

Phillip Price

Our first step is to identify how he could measure his performance improvement other than by winning. He decides that his playing statistics might be a useful guide. At the moment he can hit, on average, 12 greens in regulation and his putting average is 31 per round. Together we set goals for the next three months to increase the average number of greens hit in regulation to 14, and lower his putting average to 30. These goals are independent of any other player's performance. The weather may still play a part, but that's life.

If our goal is to win the monthly medal or reduce our handicap by 6 strokes by the end of the year, we similarly need to identify specifically what we need to do in order to have our best chance of winning. It may mean only two 3 putts per round; it may mean not risking cutting off the dog leg at the 8th or laying up on the long 12th instead of trying to reach the green in two.

Although performance goals are vital, we need to be careful in how we use them—make them as specific and independent of other people as possible.

Learning Goals

Whatever is going on in terms of our performance, there is always something we can be learning. Let's go back to how we perceive and interpret events and consider two extremes.

If we land our ball in a bunker, we will very likely interpret this as a disaster and get into all the dilemmas of trying too hard to recover. There is another way to interpret what has happened. We could see this as an opportunity to learn how to be better at getting out of bunkers. We may not have achieved our short-term goal of getting onto the green in two, but we could use the new circumstances to help us fulfill our medium-term goal to be better at bunker play.

Learning goals can be used in any circumstances—even the most adverse. The pro who is watching his score climb above 80 as he reaches the 17th tee can either blow out completely or use it as a time to learn and practice composure. It is also an opportunity to learn and practice keeping his energy level high, even under pressure.

Welshman Phillip Price had a very successful first year on the European Tour in 1991. However, when he turned professional, a lot of people thought he wasn't good enough to survive on the tour. We had been working together for a couple of years, and at the beginning of the season we set learning goals under several headings. One was to use a couple of focusing exercises that he had found particularly helpful (they are described in Chapter Five) as often as he could. Together we established a learning goal of using the exercise on every putt (instead of about half the putts). Another learning goal was not to allow himself to look to the crowd as if he were in trouble (more of this later also). Both of these goals were irrespective of the score. He was to do them as a way to improve his golf, with a view to helping his score in the medium- and long-term.

Phillip found that he played his best when he was busy with improving his game (his learning goals) rather than when he was concerned with his score (his performance). He pursued his learning goals and played better golf as a result.

When shown these paragraphs for approval, Phillip commented, "There was also another important learning goal for me. In the last year I've also learned how to be with players like Ian Woosnam and not be frightened. In the past I would go out to play feeling very nervous if I was drawn to play with a person of that stature. But I realized that if I was going to improve as a player, I had to learn how to handle these situations. I decided that I would just notice what I was sensing as I played. I intended to get used to being with and playing with players of that stature. I knew I needed to if I am going to grow as a player."

If we have clear, explicit learning goals we can have a success every time we go out, and that is what increases our confidence. And the more we learn, the faster our performance improves.

GOALS AND THE LANGUAGE OF OUR BRAIN

Our goals have the most effect on us when we set them in the language that our brain understands, i.e., in terms of what we see feel and hear. If we win a tournament, that's great, but it is what we see, hear and feel as we win that influences us and drives our behavior.

A common example of this is thinking of buying a car. Just thinking of the word *car* will not have much effect on us. It's the things that come into our mind when we think about a car that have an effect on us. Some of us will see what the car will look like; we may spend time looking at brochures. To a significant degree we will base our decision to buy on how the car looks to us and how we think we will look driving it. Others of us will think about how we will feel when we drive it, or when other people look at it. And others will want a particular kind of engine noise to listen to. The word *car* has a different meaning to each of us.

Winning also has a different meaning to each of us. At the extreme, some of us think about what we will hear people say about us. Others think about what we will feel like as we walk up the 18th fairway or go into the clubhouse. And others will see an applauding crowd at the end of the day. Most of us think about our goal in some combination of these modes.

So if our goal is to be a better golfer, we first need to define how we will recognize that we are better, i.e., make the goal SMART. Then we should decide what we will see, hear and feel when we reach that SMART goal. Using our previous example:

> *"I want to be able to hit 9 out of 10 shots with a full-body turn by the end of the month. I can do 6 at the moment, and I practice 3 times a week."*

We can add to this what we think we will see, hear and feel when we achieve the goal. For instance, we might see a different shape to the flight of the ball or a lower score on our card. We might feel more relaxed in our arms or sense more energy at the end of a round or a practice session. We might hear a crisper sound as we strike the ball, or hear people telling us how much our swing has changed.

If we identify what we will be seeing, hearing and feeling when we achieve our goals, we bring those goals to life, and that makes it much easier for our brains to recognize that we are progressing and helps our subconscious take us in that direction.

REVIEWING GOALS

An essential part of making goals useful for us is to review them at regular intervals. This tells us how far along the road toward our goal we are, and whether we are even on the right road. Whenever the "due" date for a short-term goal comes up, we need to review it to check our progress, and reset the date if necessary. We need to review medium- and long-term goals at regular intervals and not wait for the due date before checking or resetting them.

"OWN GOALS"

Time and time again, I bump into a couple of very common pitfalls or misuse of goals.

Self-Inflicted Wounds

Some of us tend very strongly to beat ourselves up emotionally if we don't reach our goals. We judge ourselves very harshly and use what we call "the failure" as an excuse for all kinds of responses that simply do not help. These responses, ranging from self-criticism that causes us to lose confidence, to anger (the club-throwers and spectator-blamers), are usually a way of saying to the world, "I normally play much better than this. I am angry, so you will know I can play better." It results in us getting very little pleasure from the game.

Potatoes

Here is an analogy that I borrow from Stephen R. Covey, a management guru whose thinking about what makes people effective I have found very helpful. He illustrates two extremes in terms of how we tackle goal setting.

Imagine we were trying to grow potatoes (or learn a new golf swing). We want to give the seeds the best chance of survival, so we plant them in fertile soil one day. What many of us do is dig them up again the next day, to check on how the roots are doing. We do the same thing day after day, and so the roots are never able to take hold. At the other extreme are those of us who never dig them up to check on progress. We never know whether they have any disease or are growing correctly until it is too late.

Let's think about how this manifests itself in golf. In the first approach, we constantly evaluate ourselves against our goals after every shot. We judge our success or failure too soon, and never give our concentration time to deepen. We recognize these golfers by the amount of self-criticism they give themselves. They are frequently to be heard saying to themselves "yes, but" or "if only." They are often frustrated with their progress and sometimes even angry with themselves.

In the second approach, we don't check where we are against our goals often enough, and the result is that we can be way off course before we even know it. We recognize these golfers by the way they are still working on fixing their swing five years into their golf game. (I don't mean refining, I mean fixing!) They will likely continue to work on an area of their game long past the point where it is helpful. They never know when to stop because they never check on their progress

Goals should be used as road signs along the way. They tell us the direction we want to go in and how we will know when we get there. They also tell us the direction we are actually heading in and how far toward that point we have progressed. And that is all. How far we have gone toward them is rarely an indication of our potential to play the game of golf.

KEY POINTS — CHAPTER FIVE

- Our ability to focus attention can be developed.

- Focusing our attention is a way to manage the stimuli entering our performance loop.

- We can focus our attention by noticing or being interested in some detail of what we are doing right now.

- Focused attention is as important between shots as during them.

- Our imagination is a very powerful tool that can be used in a constructive way.

Managing the Stimuli

Now that we have a clearer idea of where we want to go, it is time to increase our experience of what is happening right now so that our subconscious can do its job of making the appropriate corrections for us. We can do this by managing the stimuli that we interpret, which then generate our reaction.

Think of it as if our brain works like a video recorder. When the record button is pushed, all sights and sounds that we experience are recorded on the video tape. When the tape is played back, we get a high-quality image and sound. Imagine if, when the record button is pushed, we were also able to push down the play button at the same time. Not only would we record the sights and sounds coming from outside the camera (the external stimuli), we would also record again the previous sights and sounds. When we came to play back the "master" tape, the quality of the new recording would be awful.

That is what the learning process is like for a lot of us. What we perceive is so distorted and jumbled by our beliefs, assumptions and fears that the resulting recording we try to play back is jumbled and distorted. What we "see" and therefore act on is not an accurate representation of reality. And as we said before, garbage in = garbage out.

What this means to us is that the more we can ensure that the input into our brains is quality input, the more chance we have of getting quality output. And we do that by managing the stimuli that come into our performance loop.

FOCUSING ATTENTION—QUIETING THE MIND

I had always thought of concentration or focused attention as something we either had or didn't have. It was in our genes. One of the most important lessons for me as I searched for ways to raise performance was that focusing attention is a trainable skill.

In focusing our attention, several things happen at the same time. We manage the stimuli that are coming in to our performance loop so that what gets through triggers the right reaction. As we do this, the interference that is sometimes present in our mind is reduced because

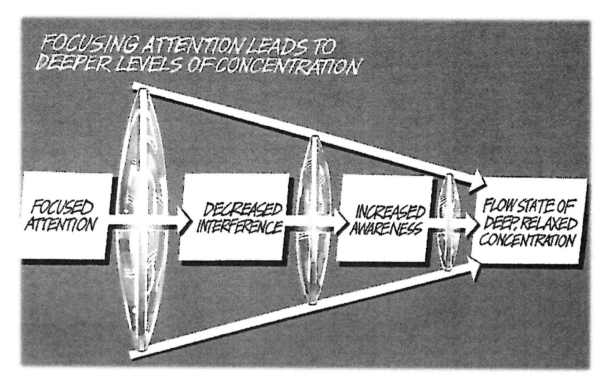

FOCUSING ATTENTION LEADS TO DEEPER LEVELS OF CONCENTRATION

FOCUSED ATTENTION → DECREASED INTERFERENCE → INCREASED AWARENESS → FLOW STATE OF DEEP RELAXED CONCENTRATION

Focused attention—how it works .

we cannot pay attention to the internal stimuli and the external stimuli at the same time. Our awareness of what we are doing increases, and the quality of what we are experiencing, i.e., the stimuli entering our brain, is higher, so our learning rate speeds up or our level of performance of the skills we already have increases.

One of the easiest ways to help ourselves focus our attention is to harness something we are all born with—curiosity. If we think about it, we all have it. When we walk down the street and see someone pointing up to the roof of a building, we always look up to see what they are so interested in. Our curiosity as human beings can be almost insatiable.

The essence of a focusing exercise in golf is to ask ourselves to notice some detail about what we are doing. In order to notice that thing, we have to focus even more of our attention on it. The simplest example of this kind of exercise I have seen was devised by Timothy Gallwey.

BACK-HIT (THE BOUNCE-HIT OF GOLF)

The back-hit exercise, to me, is a focusing exercise that has the highest probability of making the most difference to the greatest number of people. What I ask people to do is this:

"At the moment your club gets to the top or the limit of your backswing, say "back" out loud. When your club meets the ball (i.e., the moment of impact), say "hit" out loud. Don't worry about where the ball goes or how you hit it."

Most people, when they first attempt to do this, will say the words "back" and "hit" after the actual events—they say "back" when their club is already moving forwards and "hit" after the ball has already left their club face. In many cases they don't say "hit" until the ball has traveled about 30 yards!

The dialogue usually continues in this way:

"Did you say 'back' when the club got to the top of the backswing and 'hit' when it met the ball?"

"Yes, I think so."

"That's interesting, because to me it sounded as if you said both the 'back' and the 'hit' after those events occurred."

"Really?"

"Well, let's try it again. Go back and check whether or not that was actually the case."

The back-hit exercise devised by Timothy Gallwey.

As they hit the next few balls, they are busy noticing whether they say the "back" and "hit" on time (i.e., as those events actually happen). Now their attention on what they are doing increases.

"Yes, you are right!"

"Put some more attention on saying the 'back' and 'hit' and less on the other things you are trying to think about. Do you see the ball when the club strikes it?"

"No."

"Then how do you know when to say 'hit'"?

Now they realize that they don't have their full attention on the exercise.

"Find out what you are looking at if it isn't the ball."

As they try to notice what they see, their attention focuses much more specifically on their visual sense and what they actually "see." As a result they are much less caught up in trying to swing correctly, avoiding trouble, etc. Their minds become calm and quiet, the interference goes down, their experience of what is actually happening goes up, and their performance improves (see Chapter 2). They are no longer trying to do something they think they cannot do (hit a good shot), which is threatening for them. Instead they are now trying to do something they think they can do (just notice where their attention is). This reduces the threat, helps produce the "flow" state, and allows the subconscious to do its work.

Sometimes when people do this exercise the pitch and tone of their voices change dramatically. In fact, when they say "back-hit" on their practice swing, they will use a very even, relaxed tone of voice. When they say it as they hit the ball, it comes out very loud and strangled, because some of their attention is still caught up on other things. I then suggest that they say "back" and "hit" in the same way as when they practice swing.

Now their attention is caught up with something they can control—their voice—rather than something they can't control—their swing. And again they will hit the ball better. Of course it will not work this way for everyone, but it can help nine out of ten players when they are not playing well.

As a focusing exercise, this can be and indeed has been used on any shot from the driver to the putter, and by any level of player from beginner to professional. What is hard to believe or trust is that by getting our attention focused, the subconscious will make the necessary swing corrections that enable us to hit the ball better. Sometimes beginners can swing correctly without even understanding what they are doing differently. That's how powerful our brain is.

ALTERNATIVE FOCUSES

We can use an almost infinite number of focuses to streamline our attention, and they all help us to manage the stimuli coming into our brains, which can deepen our experience of what is happening right now—the present. The more accurate our experience of what our senses are telling us right now, the more learning takes place; and the more learning that takes place, the better our performance is. So here are some other ways we might get our attention focused. We can often classify them into sensory groupings.

Visual Focus

The Ball. Though not new, it is often lost because it is so obvious. Noticing what our eyes are seeing as we swing the club helps keep the video recorder in "record" mode and the play button switched off. We don't try to see anything in particular, we are merely passive observers; we simply notice what our eyes are registering.

Broad or Narrow. Some people find it useful to narrow their attention down to some very specific small detail of their visual field, such as the writing on the ball (the letters that make up the manufacturer's name) or the shape and arrangement of the dimples on the ball around the maker's logo. Others find it more helpful to have a broad focus. Here our attention would be on taking in a broad view of what our eyes are registering rather than just a small part of it. We might see the ball and the grass surrounding it.

The Hole. Watching the hole rather than the ball can be a useful exercise when putting. When we throw a ball at a target, our instinct is to look at the target—not the ball—and this can be effective in putting also. Looking at the hole as we putt can take our conscious thought away from the stroke itself and enable our subconscious to do what we have already programmed it to do.

Color. This might seem strange at first. I had asked the touring pro Richard Boxall, "What's it like when you play well?" I was looking for clues to what triggered his peak performance state. His response was "It's sort of blue." I asked him what happened whenever he thought of the color blue. He said he felt more energized and enthusiastic, and less fearful. So I suggested that he think about or see the color blue when he feels his game needs a lift. He successfully used this technique some years ago in the last tournament of the season, the Portuguese Open, when he had to hole his final putt on the final hole of the final round to save himself from a visit to the tour qualifying school.

Kinesthetic Focus

Smiling. Forcing ourselves to smile as we hit the ball has to be one of the most embarrassing exercises on the golf course. Had I not seen it work, I would never have believed it could. I was watching an 18-handicapper struggle desperately to hit the ball straight. He was trying so hard to hit the ball well that he was grimacing.

He hadn't been able to get into any exercise so far, so I thought this called for drastic measures. I asked him to smile when he hit the ball. No matter how he hit it or where he hit it, he was to keep a smile on his face for the duration of his swing. It was so ridiculous it worked! It changed the stimuli coming into the brain, and so he reacted differently. His muscles relaxed—they had to for him to smile. But it wasn't just his facial muscles. It was his arms and chest and legs as well. Remember, if we are playing badly, then we really have nothing to lose in trying this kind of exercise.

Richard Boxall

(opposite) David Feherty

"On putting...

When your mind is so absorbed with the physical action of making the putting stroke [i.e., when the video recorder is in play mode], it's unlikely that you will ever move the putter away from the ball smoothly. When this happened I would usually miss the putt. In order to overcome this I needed to divert my mind's attention away from the physical task of producing a stroke and focus instead on some other simple task, one which I could be sure of doing successfully while I played. So I decided that as I made my stroke I would try to read as many letters of the manufacturer's name printed on the ball as I could. The more letters I could read, the smoother I found my stroke became, and eventually the concentration that I applied to doing this overcame the anxiety I had previously felt about the putt itself. In other words, my mind was now so busy concentrating on reading the letters on the ball—the video recorder was in "record" mode—that it couldn't possibly interfere with the execution of the stroke."

David Feherty

Breathing Out. Exhaling as we move the club toward the ball (not as we take it away) encourages our muscles to relax and also reduces anxiety (that's where the expression "take a deep breath and ..." comes from). It seems to be most useful if the exhalation lasts for the duration of the forward swing of the club. Trying to do this for the whole of our swing is difficult, to say the least—it could be terminal if you have a very slow swing! Some people find it useful to make the breath very forceful—they blow it out. Others find it better to make it a soft breath. Experimenting will tell you what works for you.

Feeling Our Body - 1. Paying attention to how our body feels can provide some very useful ways to focus our attention and increase our experience of what we are doing, particularly because golf is so much about feeling what we are doing, or kinesthetic awareness.

David Feherty again provides a useful example of how we can do this. Every so often David has felt he has had problems with his putting, and one of the ways in which he eliminates these problems is to increase his awareness of what his body is doing as he putts (this is not necessarily a conscious awareness). He wants to make sure that his subconscious (i.e., his computer) is getting good-quality input.

He would practice putts from different positions on the putting green, and I would ask him:

"What part of your body are you most aware of as you hit the putt?"

A typical response would be "My hands." I would then push him a little further:

"Just notice your hands and be aware of what they are doing. Tell me what is it about your hands that grabs your attention."

He might say, "It's a sensation in the first two fingers of my right hand."

"Notice when that sensation begins and ends in your putting stroke."

When we had done this for about five minutes on his hands, we would repeat the same process on his arms, legs, head, trunk, etc. Our purpose was not to analyze consciously what he was doing wrong. It was to keep his mind quiet and focused so that the input to his subconscious was of much higher quality. It was to help him manage the stimuli coming into his system. In a sense we were recalibrating his feel of the shot.

Of course, this process of focusing on the sensations in our body can be used on any shot in the game. It's important to realize that what we think the shot should feel like is not what we are worried about in this exercise. We can imagine what we want to feel like before we practice each shot (more about mental rehearsal soon), but here we are trying only to be more aware of what the sensations actually are.

Feeling Our Body - 2. Putting with our eyes closed is another way to increase feel. Our visual sense is a great suppressor of feeling. When we lose one of our senses, the others automatically sharpen up to compensate, and if we close our eyes as we putt we become much more aware of the other sensations in our body. We can extend this exercise into calibrating our feel for distance and direction as follows.

Auditory Focuses

Humming. This is similar to the breathing-out exercise. If we take a practice swing at the ball and at the same time hum one note, the sound will come out in an even pitch. If we try to do the same thing when we hit the ball, the sound comes out with a lot more emphasis in the middle of it. If we make sure that our voice stays even as we swing through the ball, we will likely make a much smoother swing. To keep our voice even, we have to relax our muscles, and it can be easier to keep the sound of our voice even than to relax our muscles.

Impact Sound. Every time the club meets the ball it makes a sound that is likely to be different on each shot. We can listen for how the sound varies from shot to shot. It may have a different pitch each time, it may be a long or a short sound, or it may be loud or quiet. We may even hear the sound of the club moving through the air.

Between Shots

So far we have been talking about the things we can focus on as we play each shot. But most of the time in golf is not spent playing shots. It is spent walking and waiting for our turn to play. It is therefore important for us to manage the stimuli or keep our minds quiet in these in-between periods.

We can do this in the same way that we did as we played the shots. Here are some examples of what we might focus our attention on as we walk or wait between shots. Always bear in mind that different focuses work for different people. You have to experiment to find out yours.

Visual. The trees, crowd, colors of what we are looking at. The breadth or narrowness of our visual field—do we look down at our feet or do we have a broad view of the crowd or landscape? The shape of the next shot we want to play.

Kinesthetic. How does our body feel when we are walking? Do particular sensations stand out? Is our walk smooth or jerky, flexible or tight, relaxed or tense, balanced or unbalanced? Do we feel the right side more than the left. Which part of us is warmest? Do we feel the strength of any of these sensations? What does our breathing feel like?

Auditory. What does our breath sound like? What other noises can we hear—the wind, crowd noise, motors running? How loud is what we hear? Does it change its pitch, tone, rhythm, tempo, direction?

There are three useful questions to apply to each of these focuses to help us keep our attention:

What do I notice? What specifically is easiest for me to notice about what my senses are telling me right now? Is it something I see, feel or hear?

When or where do I notice it? When in the duration of the swing or when between the shots do I notice it? Where in my body do I notice it?

How much of it do I notice? What is the intensity of the thing I have noticed? A lot, a little, a medium amount?

Colin Montgomerie, using his imagination by acting as if ...

These apply both as we are playing a shot or between shots. Trying to answer these questions forces us to pay more attention to the object of our attention; i.e., it focuses our attention.

IMAGINATION

Our imagination has an extraordinarily powerful effect on our performance. It can be both positive or negative, depending on what we are imagining. When we experience interference, it is usually our imagination at work. In trying to anticipate what the future will be, we often imagine the worst. We found out with the pendulum experiment in Chapter 1 that whatever is in our mind is reflected physically in some way—however small. Mental rehearsal and imagery techniques harness this principle in a positive way and are used by many leading athletes (and business people). They can be very powerful if we let ourselves get fully into them.

IMAGERY

Acting as if ...

1. Think about what your posture is like when you play well. Compare it with what it is like when you play badly. Most people hang their head and slouch when they aren't on top of their game. It is a reflection or representation of what is happening in their mind— their mental state. We can prevent ourselves becoming like this, or change things when we are like this, by maintaining our "winning" posture no matter how we are playing or acting as if we were winning. We walk with our head up at the same pace and rhythm as if we were playing well. We hold the club the same way, we breathe the same way, we do everything exactly the same way as when we are playing well, no matter the result. Keeping his attention on the feel of his "winning" posture was one way that Phillip Price kept his composure in his first season as a professional.

2. Second, we could think of a quality or attitude that we would like to exhibit as we play. For example, we might want to swing more smoothly, or play with a more positive attitude. What we do is act as if we had this quality or attitude. It is as if we are acting the whole thing out before a movie camera. We need to exaggerate or ham up what we are doing for the camera. The key is to get so engrossed in the role play that it becomes real. The more we get into the acting, the closer our mental state gets to the one we want—and our actions will follow.

I've Done It Before.

David Hemery won the gold medal for the 400 meters hurdles in the 1968 Olympic Games in Mexico. Years later, I asked him, "Did it feel strange when you were out there running the final?" "No," he replied. "In my mind I had rehearsed that race many times. I knew every step I was going to take, and so it was easy."

Sometimes you can't act as if...

3. When we are putting we could imagine that the hole is the size of a bucket. Putting into a hole of this size reduces the threat we perceive and allows our muscles to relax. We only have to be "in" the exercise for the few seconds of making the putt.

4. On any shot, short or long, we could imagine that we are 30 pounds heavier, as if we would sink into the ground and can feel our weight pressing down onto our ankles. Or we can imagine we are 30 pounds lighter so that we are so light we can barely feel the ground beneath us, and if there were a wind, we would blow away. The aim, as always, is to get our attention focused. Although the object of focus may seem irrelevant, it works well for some golfers.

5. We pretend that our club has a brain and talent all of its own—that it is the most well trained, experienced and capable club in the world. It knows what to do and how to swing; all we have to do is let it show us how. We do nothing but allow the club to show us what "it wants to do"!

So far, all these focusing exercises have been things we can do while we are actually playing our golf. However, there are also things we can do before we even get out on the golf course that can make a significant difference to the way we play.

Mental Rehearsal

Every time we visualize a movement in our mind, it causes tiny little impulses to travel down our nerves into the relevant muscles and produce the movement in miniature. Each time an impulse travels down to a muscle, it makes it slightly easier for the next impulse to travel down the same route between our brain and our body. It is as if a groove is being cut (some people refer to it as building muscle memory). The more we image something over and over in our mind, the easier it becomes to do that thing.

Here is a way to go about mentally rehearsing our golf. Sit in a chair or lie on the floor; and get comfortable and breathe normally. Keep your hands and feet uncrossed and close your eyes. Get as relaxed as possible (when you do this you change the brain wave to a slower frequency that is much more conducive for learning).

Each time you exhale, mentally count from 10 to 1, one number on each exhalation. Form an image in your mind of whatever it is you want to do, perform or learn, and experience yourself doing it. In your mind's eye see, hear and feel it in as much detail as possible as if it is happening to you right now. Allow yourself to enjoy the exercise and get into the experience as much as you can. If it's a swing, play it over

The One That Got Away

We often get back to the clubhouse and tell everyone about the shot we dumped into the water at the 15th. If what we think about over and over is reflected in our actions, what are we rehearsing for the next time we play that hole?

Visualizing—useful mental rehearsal.

Basketball

A classic piece of research was carried out with basketball players. They were divided into three groups. One did no practice at shooting free throws. The second did ordinary shooting. The third did only mental rehearsal. The first group made no improvement, the second significant improvement, and the third made the same improvement as the second group. Those doing only mental rehearsal improved as much as those doing the physical practice.

and over in your mind. If it's an attitude, imagine what you would see/hear/feel if you had that attitude.

When you feel ready (give it at least a few minutes), mentally count on each exhalation from 1 to 10. As you get to 10, open your eyes and come back to the room you are sitting in.

Like all techniques, some of us will find mental rehearsal easier than others, but like most skills, it gets easier with practice.

(Opposite) One man's stimulation...
Phillip Price sinks winning put to defeat
Phil Mickelson during the 34th Ryder Cup.

KEY POINTS — CHAPTER SIX

- Practice makes permanent.

- Knowledge and desire are important factors in practice.

- Practice:
    With clear goals
    A little and often
    What you will do when you play
    Both sides of our brain
    The wrong way sometimes.

- Use a diary to stay on track.

- Reward yourself when you succeed.

- Commit!

Practice Makes Permanent

"Practice makes perfect." What a great saying. It is not true, but it is a great saying. Hasn't that been drummed into us throughout our lives?

"No one ever became a great player without practice." Now that I can agree with. But there are hundreds of professional golfers—and thousands of amateurs—who have been out on the practice ground until their hands have blistered, and they have never improved their score. Why is this? Because we have got only part of the story.

Practice makes permanent. I'll say it again, but louder!

Practice makes permanent.

Whatever we do over and over again becomes a habit. So if we are not getting the improvement we want in our game, then we are not repeating the appropriate behavior. Here are three elements I find useful when thinking about practice.

1. Knowledge	what to do and why to do it
2. Skill	mastery of what to do
3. Desire	want, or commitment to what to do

For our practice to be effective, we need to know what we should be practicing, and why we should practice it. If we don't understand why we are practicing, then it can make it very hard to generate the high energy we need for "high performing" or quality practice. We develop the skill through repetition of the components of that skill in low-pressure situations. From that come our results.

Knowledge and desire, together with practice, build skills. Skill and practice together produce results. Results reinforce our desire and thirst for knowledge. (See diagram page 97)

LOBOTOMIES

At the beginning of this book we said that it is not possible to separate the mental from the physical without a lobotomy. No mental

Tiger Woods
Practice makes perfect?

state means no physical activity. Comatose! So anytime we practice, we are making both the physical and the mental parts of our game habitual.

For instance, when we shake our head after each shot and then try harder to get our swing right the next time, we ingrain the habit of trying harder as well as improving the swing. Therefore we should not be surprised when we do the same thing when we get out on the course.

Much of the practice I see is of marginal value to the golfers because it lacks organization. I have worked with several tour pros who complained of problems with their putting or short game. As we investigated the causes, we discovered that they hardly practiced this part of their game. It wasn't surprising that they weren't putting well; they hardly ever set foot on the practice putting green. Organizing our practice in terms of accurate knowledge of what to do, and how to do it, can make a huge difference in how productive it is for us. So let's explore some ideas about what to practice and how.

GOAL SETTING IN PRACTICE

As always, the first step in improvement is to decide which direction we want to go in and how to recognize it when we get there. With some careful thought we can set SMART goals not only for each practice session, but also to encompass the different parts of a practice session. Why so much detail? Because every time we achieve a goal it sends a message to our subconscious that we are succeeding, and this is what builds our self-confidence (or removes our self-doubt). Some examples in Chapter 4 on goal setting will show you how we might go about doing this.

Most golfers I meet know what they want to achieve but have not addressed a fundamental decision they need to make: Are they willing to pay the price to achieve that goal? To achieve anything worthwhile takes effort. It can be fun and rewarding, but at the same time it does take sustained effort. Most amateurs and a lot of pros look for quick fixes, which are usually much more difficult to sustain.

Think for a moment about what we would do if we wanted to increase the strength in our right arm. We would lift small weights on a regular basis until the muscles in our arms adapt. When we first start training it feels very uncomfortable, and a voice in the back of our mind tries to tell us that we can put off the training until tomorrow, or maybe that we can do without it altogether. We continue because we know that if we do, we will grow stronger. This is how it is with all skills. We have to be willing to pay the price—whatever that may be—if we want to achieve our goals. During the years it took Nick Faldo to remodel his swing with David Leadbetter, his results were so poor that people questioned whether or not he had made the right decision.

The price we have to pay is usually one or the other or both of the following:

- an investment of time to build or refresh our skills (amateurs particularly often don't even get out on the practice ground);
- a change in behavior that will feel unfamiliar and even uncomfortable for some people.

Most of us resist change. We prefer to remain and feel more comfortable with the familiar and the known, even if it is not producing the result we want. (Better the devil we know than the devil we don't know.) Yet implicit in improvement is change and doing things differently. If we are not willing to pay the price, then let's decide that at the outset and change our expectations of what we want out of our golf.

By the way, if you learned to walk and talk, you have the ability to learn to play this game. You may not play in the Open, but you can certainly have fun. And if at the moment you are not improving and not enjoying your golf, you are either practicing the wrong things or aren't willing to pay the price.

I believe the brain is like a muscle—like any other, it can be improved.

Tennis superstar Ivan Lendl

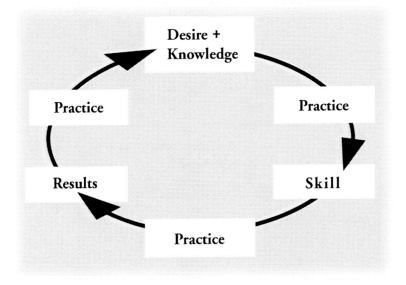

Practice makes permanent.

Smarter, Not Harder

Several touring pros have cut down the amount they practice to 100 balls a day. This was as a result of discovering that the quality of their attention was poor after that many balls. They became bored, and their practice became counterproductive. Of course the price they had to pay was the discomfort of everyone telling them that they would never improve if they didn't work harder. They decided it was more useful to work smarter.

PLAYING GOLF VS BUILDING A SWING

Most of the practice I see golfers of all levels do goes like this. They stand on the range with about 100 balls and hit them one after the other, with a few practice swings in between. It is a great way to learn to swing the club correctly (given some of the caveats we have explored in this book). But then they become puzzled when they find it hard to sustain what they did in practice when they are out on the course playing golf. It's often because they have failed to understand the difference between developing the skills—what is often called the "muscle memory"—and implementing the skills in the competitive environment—playing golf. They are different and demand different forms of practice.

Building a Swing

If we are interested in building a swing or effecting some change in our swing, we need to get the maximum number of repetitions with the highest intensity of experiencing those repetitions. We want to "burn" the movement into our brain. Hitting lots of balls is invaluable, provided we can do it with the minimum of self-criticism and evaluation. The more we just notice what is happening, the faster things will change.

Lots of short practice sessions are much more useful than fewer lengthy ones. Pausing after every ten or so shots doesn't overload our attention span. One hour's quality practice four days a week is much more useful than four hours' practice once a week.

Playing Golf

Beating balls as a means of practicing our swing is useful, but it isn't golf. In fact, when we spend a lot of time practicing this way, we are forming a habit we will never use on the golf course, i.e., hitting one shot after the other from the same spot with the same club. When we play the game we do the opposite. We play each shot from a different location, with a different club, and we have on average 2.5 minutes between each shot. This means we need to become skilled at bringing our concentration together every 2.5 minutes. There is no way we will sustain peak concentration for the 4+ hours it takes to play 18 holes.

As far as practicing in a way that is valuable in terms of improving our performance out on the course, we need to create a more realistic set of circumstances, and practice what we will be doing when we get out on the course. Once our swing is built to some degree, we

The Langer limbo—withstands the pressure of the Ryder Cup!

could practice using a different club for each shot, with at least a one-minute interval between each swing. Playing from a different location each time is usually problematic, but we can at least aim at different targets on each shot and try different shapes on each shot as if we were playing a hole.

We can take this a stage further, and imagine that we are playing our home course. For example, if the first hole is a par-4, and we normally take a 3-wood from the tee, we pick our target and hit the 3-wood. We watch the flight of the ball and try to imagine where it would have come to rest if we had actually been playing the first hole. Then, on the basis of how well we hit our "tee-shot," we could plan our second shot that we would have left to the green. If we hit a good 3-wood, then our next shot might be with a 9-iron, so we take our 9-iron, and imagine playing the ball right down the flag. If we pushed our 3-wood, we might decide that we need to manufacture a cut-shot around a tree in order to get onto the green, and so we try to conjure up a left-to-right shot, and so on. In theory, we could play a full 18 holes like this, and in doing so we would be practicing the focusing and imaging skills we have been discussing in previous chapters.

In putting, we could place four balls in a circle, each ball being 6 inches from the hole. We putt them all. Assuming we sink them all, we replace them at 1-foot intervals around the hole and do the same again. We repeat the process, placing the balls at ever greater distances until we miss one. At this point we go back to the beginning and start the process all over again. Let's say that we missed the 15th putt.

"

Pressure

I believe that the ability to withstand pressure comes with experience. It's a learning process, but it is possible to manipulate your mind to such a degree that you forget about the circumstances. Difficult though it is [when you are under pressure], you try to clear your mind of the fact that a shot or a putt is important.

On the 18th green at Kiawah, I just followed my usual routine. I studied the line, and once I had a clear picture in my mind of the ball heading along that line to the hole, I committed myself totally to the putt and concentrated on the speed. Even if it turns out to be a bad read, it's always better to pick a definite line and stick to it. You make a much better stroke when you do that. The importance of developing and then adhering to a pre-shot routine cannot be overstated. You should develop your own style— not just on the green, but for all shots—and then stick to it. And all the time that I'm surveying a putt, my concentration and awareness are increasing.

"

Bernhard Langer

Imagine what it will be like when we get to the 15th putt on the next series of putts. The pressure gets much closer to that experienced in competitive play. And that's what we are trying to practice.

What we practice becomes a habit. That's why it is important to make at least a part of our practice as close to the real thing as we can.

RIGHT BRAIN IT

We discussed right and left brain theory earlier in the book. I want to remind you at this stage that our practice time can be used to build our skill at whichever side of our brain needs developing. The left-brainers could be practicing and getting used to letting go and thinking less about their shot as they swing. The right-brainers could be going through a thorough pre-shot routine and practicing working out their yardage.

JOURNALS

Many touring pros keep a journal of what they do on the golf course and what happens inside them as they play each round—particularly within respect to what they see, hear and feel as they play and what the result of what they saw, heard and felt was. Then, when I meet up with them, we look back over a few weeks of note-taking and search for any trends. It is one of the ways in which we discover the cause of a problem shot: sometimes it's just the lack of practice time given to that shot; other times it might be their dominant way of approaching the game—right- or left-brained or dominant sensory mode. Keeping a diary is a useful way to keep ourselves on track.

WHEN WRONG IS RIGHT

When we practice, most of us are obsessed with swinging the club in the "correct" way—whatever our version of that is—and quite rightly so. But there are times when practicing the wrong thing is actually doing the right thing. For example, imagine we are trying to increase our awareness or feel on our short pitches. It can be helpful to experiment and execute it in all kinds of "wrong" ways, such as a stance that is too open to the target line, or a clubface that is too open or closed to the ball. We may never want to execute the shot this way when we play, but doing so in practice increases our experience base. We feel new sensations, and our awareness of what we can do with our body and the club increases. In essence we are exaggerating the shot to expand our range of awareness. We don't spend all our practice time doing this, just enough to have fun with it.

REWARD SYSTEMS

All good coaches and managers know that the most effective way to make any behavior a habit is to reward the behavior each time it happens. So when we swing the club the way the pro wants us to, he or she will praise us. Each time we do something the pro likes, we get a reward—our ego gets stroked. We like the "payoff" of the compliment, and so we seek to get more compliments by repeating the same behavior. We expect others, especially coaches, to "reward" us in some way when we do something well.

We can harness this effect by setting up reward systems for ourselves, without waiting for the coach or anyone else to do it for us. We tell our subconscious that it did a great job for us by giving ourselves something we want when we achieve a specific goal. It needs to be something we would not do in the normal course of events so that it stands out as a reward.

Greg Norman

Reward the Right Behavior

While on holiday, the 10-year-old son of a friend of mine idly put his hand into the coin return slot of a public telephone and found a coin. The rest of the holiday was spent searching every public telephone he saw to see if there were any coins left behind. His behavior had been rewarded and was subsequently repeated—and how.

Here is an example from a tour pro:

Goal	Reward
Complete my learning goals for the week.	6 new music CDs
Finish in the top thirty.	12 new music CDs
Finish in the top ten.	New stereo system
Win the tournament.	New Porsche

Now of course the rewards for us would look a lot different from these (well, most of us, anyway). And it does not have to be expensive or even cost anything. However, it does need to be something which we recognize we would not ordinarily have done for ourselves.

Many of us fend off the potential reward. How often have you heard someone dismiss a compliment by saying, "Oh it was nothing," or "I was lucky. I don't normally hit my driver that straight." We also say to ourselves, "I don't need to reward myself specifically. I know when I have done well."

We can set up reward systems for our practice as well as our competitive play. Completing the goals for a week's practice may deserve the book we wanted to buy, or a beer with our friends. We do, however, need to be careful. Used inappropriately, encouragement or rewards can also cause us to move into the trying-too-hard mode. We can become too attached to pleasing our coach, or getting the "present," and as a consequence get overanxious about the results.

COMMITMENT

Commitment is like concentration in that we all use the word, we all think we know what we mean, and we all find it very hard to do. Yet nothing happens without it. Unless we are committed to our plan of action, then we are not going to stay with it, and nothing will change.

Most of the high performers I have encountered—both in sports and in business—attribute a high proportion of their success to their level of commitment to what they are doing. Commitment in golf is generated in the same way as anything else—by a strong desire for the game, or some aspect of it.

We become committed when we are very clear about our purpose in playing golf. By purpose I mean the reason why we play—the payoff for us. By the way, even for the top golfers the payoff has usually more to do with pride of performance than money. Even though the

> *Whatever you can do or dream you can do, begin it. Boldness has genius, power and magic in it. Begin it now.*

Goethe

financial payoff is sometimes huge, it is the pursuit of excellence that most of them are after.

The less clear we are about whether we really want to be playing in this tournament today, or spend an afternoon on the practice ground, or even go out at all, the more difficult it is for us to put our energy into what we are doing. Commitment starts with a vision of our innermost desire, a dream, an admission of our innermost wants; and it builds as we translate it into action.

Successful people usually have a vision that fires them up so much it becomes an irresistible force. We've all heard about or know people who display a tremendous commitment to doing something that really matters to them. I know of several young golfers who are happy to make an eight-hour journey so that they can get 90 minutes' tuition with their favorite coach. Their commitment to their vision of being great golfers is total. Others spend hours working on their putting on the practice green while their friends go out for a game on the course. They are prepared to make sacrifices to do something that fits in with their vision—to be a better golfer. If we want to improve, we must demonstrate a similar degree of commitment.

In discussing commitment in the business world with a very good friend of mine, I described to him how I sometimes test a golfer's commitment. He suggested that one way to think about commitment is to ask ourselves: "What if I had to do that thing? What if not doing it wasn't an option?" As I asked myself those questions I began to realize that it forced me to consider possibilities that I had been avoiding.

Let's look at a real example. Several years ago I was working with David Feherty, who for some reason was quitting on his shots in the downswing. He couldn't seem to commit himself to release the clubhead freely through the ball. On the practice ground he was fine, but when playing in a tournament he would quit a fraction of a second before impact, with the result that he would push the ball out to the right. Each time we would meet, he would say that he really meant to commit to the shot, but he didn't seem to be able to "stay with it" when the pressure was on.

So I asked him, "If I threatened to blow your brains out if you quit on any shot, would you stay committed?"

The reply was "Absolutely."

Then I altered my approach slightly and asked him, "If I promised you £50,000 if you committed fully on each shot irrespective of where the ball went, would you take it?"

His response was immediate. "Absolutely. I would make more

Until one is committed, there is hesitancy, the chance to draw back, always ineffectiveness, concerning all acts of initiative (and creation). There is one elementary truth, the ignorance of which kills countless ideas and splendid plans: the moment when one definitely commits oneself, then providence moves too. All sorts of things occur to help one that would never have otherwise occurred A whole stream of events issues from the decision, raising in one's favor all manner of unforeseen incidents and meetings and material assistance which no man could have dreamt would have come his way.

From The Scottish Himalayan Expedition by W. H. Murray

Commitment—
Stephen Ames style!

money doing that than winning this week. And I wouldn't even have to make the cut."

"So committing is within your control if you absolutely had to do it?"

"Yes, I suppose it is," he said.

"OK, David, how much money can you afford to lose?"
He started to say £1000 (things were different in those days) and then smelled a rat.

"Five hundred pounds!"

"Here's an idea. Given that you have said that if you had to, you would commit on every single shot, how about writing a check to your favorite charity for £1000 and leaving it with me. If you commit on every shot in the next week, I will return it you. If I think that for whatever reason you quit even on one shot, I will send the check off. Of course your money would not be in any danger, because you have said this is within your conscious control if the stakes are high enough (the stakes being loads of money or getting your head blown off). It will only be in danger if you don't mean to do what it takes to commit."

Now of course he faced the prospect of quitting and losing money, never mind not earning any by missing the cut. He would be much better off committing.

I then added: "David, only say yes to this if you are sure you can do it. Once you sign the check, the deal is on and only negotiable with my agreement."

If this sounds harsh to you, it was. But David and I had worked together for some time and there was a high level of trust between us. And the choice to do it was entirely his. Thinking this was a painful but useful exercise to try out, he duly wrote a check for £1000 to the Royal Society for the Prevention of Cruelty to Animals. He also called me a few unrepeatable names as he left.

When I met David again one week later, I was talking to the new Italian Open champion. He had finally understood what commitment really meant to him. And he told me to send the check off anyway!

Nothing happens without our commitment to see it through to the end.

The Last Word

For 30 years I have been involved in the vocation and business of helping people improve their performance in all kinds of activities. This book is not an attempt to capture it all; it is a collection of some things that golfers have found useful in their pursuit of peak performance.

I am frequently asked what I think are the most common reasons why people don't perform to their potential. My answer at the time of writing this book is this:

1. We don't act on what we already know. We don't do anything with the knowledge and skill we already have in our possession.

2. We are not willing to pay the price in order to realize our objectives—in particular we are unwilling to take a risk and make a mistake and learn from that mistake.

3. We are reluctant to be ruthlessly objective about whether what we do actually produces the result we want. We labor under false beliefs.

4. We don't organize ourselves properly.

To me the most effective solutions are the simple ones. As my friend would say (the one with the telephone-addict son!), "This does not have to be rocket science."

This book was born from my experiences with the golfers and others who have sought my help with their games, and who had the patience and the trust in me to endure my experiments with performance enhancement. Some of them became "casualties." They didn't survive the experiments. Sorry, folks, but I'm still learning too. Some of the survivors have been mentioned in this book.

My hope is that this book will enable you to make some sense of what is possible for your own performance, and help you find some ways to make some more steps in whatever direction you would like to go.

Happy golfing.

If you would like further information on the material in this book, and/or its application to business performance, please write to:

Insideout Development LLC
95 North 490 West
American Fork
Utah 84003
1.888.262.2448
afine@insideoutdev.com

INDEX

Page numbers in italic denote illustrations

PICTURE CREDITS